APAROKSHĀ

OR

SELF-REALI...

OF

SRI SANKARĀCHĀRYA

Text, with word-for-word Translation,
English Rendering and Comments

By
SWAMI VIMUKTANANDA

Ꮧꮻvaita Ashrama

(Publication Department)
5 Dehi Entally Road
Kolkata 700 014

Published by
Swami Mumukshananda
President, Advaita Ashrama
Mayavati, Champawat, Uttaranchal
from its Publication Department, Kolkata
Email : mail@advaitaashrama.org
Website : www.advaitaashrama.org

ISBN 81-7505-107-8

Printed in India at
Gipidi Box Co
Kolkata 700 014

PREFACE

Such treatises as aim at serving as introductions to a more advanced study of a system of philosophy are generally known as ' Prakarana Granthas.' Besides giving an outline of the system, each of them emphasizes some one or other of the main features. *Aparokshânubhuti* is one such little manual, which, while presenting a brief description of Vedanta, deals specially with that aspect of it which relates to the *realization* (Anubhuti) of the highest Truth. Such realization, unlike the knowledge of objects through sense-perception or inference, is an immediate and direct perception of one's own Self, which is here indicated by the word *Aparoksha*.

The central theme of the book is the identity of the Jivâtman (individual self) and Paramâtman (Universal Self). This identity is realized through the removal of the ignorance that hides the truth, by the light of Vichâra or enquiry alone (verse II). To enable the mind to embark on such an investigation into truth, certain disciplines are laid down, which are not peculiar to Vedanta, but are indispensable for all such enquiries into the highest Truth. The book then gives a description of one who has attained this realization and of the nature of his life. Then follows a discussion on Prârabdha, the momentum of past actions. The author contends that after realization, when ignorance with all its effects entirely disappears, the question of the survival of the body for working out Prârabdha is altogether out of place; and the Sruti sometimes speaks of it only to explain to the ignorant the apparent behaviour of a man of realization, who, so far as he himself is concerned, is ever immersed in the Supreme Truth.

Verses 100 to 129 deal specially with the fifteen stages through which the seeker after Truth passes—which, by the way, are similar to those experienced by a Râja-Yogin; but the two are entirely different. Then is the oneness of cause and effect—the Absolute and the manifested universe—which is wound up with the culminating thought of the Vedanta philosophy that all that is visible and invisible is in reality the one eternal Âtman, which is Pure Consciousness (verse 141).

The authorship of the book is generally attributed to Sri Sankarâchârya. Even if this be disputed, the teachings are undoubtedly Advaitic. To those, therefore, who have neither the time nor the opportunity to go through the classical works of Sankarâchârya, a treatise like the present one will be an invaluable guide in their quest after spiritual truths.

It may be mentioned here that verses 89 to 98 occur with slight variations also in the Nâdabindu Upanishad (21-29) and verses 102 to 136, 140 and 142, in the Tejabindu Upanishad (15-51).

Translations of the book into English and some Indian vernaculars have already been published. But the need having been expressed by some beginners for word-for-word equivalents and notes in English, a fresh attempt is being made to meet these requirements. The author acknowledges his indebtedness to the existing translations as well as to the commentary of Vidyâranya. It is hoped that the book will be of use to those for whom it is intended.

SWAMI VIMUKTANANDA

BELUR MATH,
10th September, 1938.

CONTENTS

APAROKSHÂNUBHUTI

OR

SELF-REALIZATION

श्रीहरिं परमानन्दमुपदेष्टारमीश्वरम् ।
व्यापकं सर्वलोकानां कारणं तं नमाम्यहम् ॥ १ ॥

अहं I परमानन्दं Supreme Bliss उपदेष्टारं the First Teacher
ईश्वरं Iswara (the Supreme Ruler) व्यापकं All-pervading सर्व-
लोकानां of all Lokas (worlds) कारणं Cause तं Him श्रीहरिं to Sri
Hari नमामि bow down.

1. I[1] bow down to Him—to Sri Hari (the
destroyer of ignorance), the Supreme Bliss, the
First Teacher, Iswara, the All-pervading One
and the Cause[2] of all Lokas (the universe).

[1] *I*—The ego, the Jiva in bondage, who identifies himself
with the gross, subtle and causal bodies, undergoes various
sufferings and strives for liberation.

[2] *The Cause*—The efficient as well as the material cause.
Just as a spider weaves its net from the materials of its own
body, so does Iswara create this universe out of Himself.

अपरोक्षानुभूतिर्वै प्रोच्यते मोक्षसिद्धये ।
सद्भिरेव प्रयत्नेन वीक्षणीया मुहुर्मुहुः ॥ २ ॥

मोक्षसिद्धये For the acquisition of final liberation (from
the bondage of ignorance) वै (expletive) अपरोक्षानुभूतिः (the
means of attaining to) Self-realization (अस्माभिः by us)
प्रोच्यते is spoken of in detail सद्भिः by the pure in heart एव

only (इयं this) प्रयत्नेन with all effort मुहुर्मुहुः again and again वीक्षणीया should be meditated upon.

2. Herein is expounded (the means of attaining to) Aparokshânubhuti[1] (Self-realization) for the acquisition of final liberation. Only the pure in heart should constantly and with all effort meditate upon the truth herein taught.

[1] *Aparokshânubhuti*—It is the direct cognition of the Âtman which is always present in all thought.

Everybody has some knowledge of this Âtman or Self, for, to deny the Self is to deny one's own existence. But at first its real nature is not known. Later on, when the mind becomes purer through Upâsanâ and Tapas, the veil of ignorance is gradually withdrawn and the Self begins to reveal its real nature. A higher knowledge follows at an advanced stage, when the knowledge of the 'Self as mere witness' is seen as absorbing all other thoughts.

But the end is not yet reached. The idea of duality, such as 'I am the witness' ('I' and the 'witness'), is still persisting. It is only at the last stage when the knower and the known merge in the Self-effulgent Âtman, which alone ever *is*, and besides which nothing else exists, that the culmination is reached. This realization of the *non-dual* is the consummation of Aparokshânubhuti.

It is needless to say that Aparokshânubhuti may here mean also the work that deals with it.

स्ववर्णाश्रमधर्मेण तपसा हरितोषणात् ।
साधनं प्रभवेत् पुंसां वैराग्यादिचतुष्टयम् ॥ ३ ॥

स्ववर्णाश्रमधर्मेण By the performance of duties pertaining to one's social order and stage in life तपसा by austerity हरितोषणात् by propitiating Hari (the Lord) पुंसां of men वैराग्यादि Vairâgya (dispassion) and the like चतुष्टयं the four-fold साधनं means (to knowledge) प्रभवेत् arises.

3. The four preliminary qualifications[1] (the means to the attainment of knowledge), such as Vairâgya (dispassion) and the like, are acquired by men by propitiating Hari (the Lord), through austerities and the performance of duties pertaining to their social order and stage in life.

[1] *The four preliminary qualifications*—These are वैराग्यं dispassion, विवेकः discrimination, शमादिषट्सम्पत्तिः six treasures such as Sama (the control of the mind) and the like, and मुमुक्षुत्वं yearning for liberation (from the bondage of ignorance).

ब्रह्मादिस्थावरान्तेषु वैराग्यं विषयेष्वनु ।
यथैव काकविष्ठायां वैराग्यं तद्धि निर्मलम् ॥ ४ ॥

यथैव Just as काकविष्ठायां to the excreta of a crow वैराग्यं indifference (तथैव in the same way) ब्रह्मादिस्थावरान्तेषु विषयेषु to all objects of enjoyment from Brahmaloka to this world अनु (लक्षीकृत्य) considering (their perishable nature) (यत्) वैराग्यं indifference तत् that हि verily निर्मलं pure (वैराग्यं indifference).

4. The indifference with which one treats the excreta of a crow—such an indifference to all objects of enjoyment from the realm of Brahmâ to this world (in view of their perishable nature), is verily called pure Vairâgya.[1]

[1] *Pure Vairâgya*—One may be indifferent to the enjoyments of this world only in expectation of better enjoyments in the next. This kind of indifference is tainted with desires which bar the door to Knowledge. But the indifference that results from a due deliberation on the evanescent nature of this world as well as the world to come, is alone pure, and productive of the highest good.

नित्यमात्मस्वरूपं हि दृश्यं तद्विपरीतगम् ।
एवं यो निश्चयः सम्यग्विवेको वस्तुनः स वै ॥ ५ ॥

आत्मस्वरूपं Âtman in itself हि verily नित्यं permanent दृश्यं the seen तद्विपरीतगं going against that (i.e. opposed to Âtman) एवं thus यः which सम्यक् settled निश्चयः conviction सः that वै truly वस्तुनः of thing विवेकः discrimination (ज्ञेयः is known).

5. Âtman[1] (the seer) in itself is alone permanent, the seen[2] is opposed to it (i.e. transient)—such a settled conviction is truly known as discrimination.

[1] *Atman*—In this ever-changing world there is one changeless being as witness of these changes. This permanent ever-seeing being is Âtman.

[2] *The seen*—This comprises everything other than Âtman, such as objects of the senses, the senses, the mind and the Buddhi.

सदैव वासनात्यागः शमोऽयमिति शब्दितः ।
निग्रहो बाह्यवृत्तीनां दम इत्यभिधीयते ॥ ६ ॥

सदैव At all times वासनात्यागः abandonment of desires अयं this शम इति as Sama (control of the mind) शब्दितः is termed बाह्यवृत्तीनां of the external functions of the organs निग्रहः restraint दम इति as Dama अभिधीयते is called.

6. Abandonment of desires[1] at all times is called Sama and restraint of the external functions of the organs is called Dama.

[1] *Abandonment of desires*—Previous impressions that are lying dormant in the mind as well as the contact of the mind with the external objects give rise to desires. To abandon

all desires is to dissociate the mind from these two sets of stimuli.

विषयेभ्यः परावृत्तिः परमोपरतिर्हि सा ।

सहनं सर्वदुःखानां तितिक्षा सा शुभा मता ॥ ७ ॥

विषयेभ्य: From objects (of the senses) (या which) परावृत्तिः turning away सा that हि verily परमा the highest उपरति: Uparati सर्वदुःखानां of all sorrow or pain (यत् which) सहनं endurance सा that शुभा conducive to happiness तितिक्षा forbearance मता is known.

7.   Turning away completely from all sense-objects is the height of Uparati,[1] and patient endurance of all sorrow or pain is known as Titikshâ which is conducive to happiness.

[1] *Uparati*—Apparently Uparati differs very little from Sama and Dama, yet there is a difference. While practising Sama and Dama there is an effort to restrain the mind's outgoing propensities. But in Uparati the equipoise of the mind becomes spontaneous and there is no further striving to gain it.

निगमाचार्यवाक्येषु भक्तिः श्रद्धेति विश्रुता ।

चित्तैकाग्र्यं तु सल्लक्ष्ये समाधानमिति स्मृतम् ॥ ८ ॥

निगमाचार्यवाक्येषु In the words of the Vedas and the teachers भक्ति: faith श्रद्धेति as Sraddhâ विश्रुता is known तु and सल्लक्ष्ये on the only object Sat चित्तैकाग्र्यं concentration of the mind समाधानमिति as Samâdhâna (deep concentration) स्मृतम् is regarded.

8.   Implicit faith in the words of the Vedas and the teachers (who interpret them) is known as Sraddhâ, and concentration of the mind on

the only object Sat (i.e. Brahman) is regarded as Samâdhâna.

संसारबंधनिर्मुक्तिः कथं मे स्यात् कदा विधे ।
इति या सुदृढा बुद्धिर्वक्तव्या सा मुमुक्षुता ॥ ६ ॥

(हे) विधे O Lord कदा when कथं how मे my संसारबंधनिर्मुक्तिः the final liberation from the bonds of the world (i.e. births and deaths) स्यात् will be इति या such सुदृढा strong बुद्धिः desire सा that मुमुक्षुता Mumukshutâ (yearning for final liberation) वक्तव्या should be called.

9.   When and how shall I, O Lord, be free from the bonds of this world (i.e. births and deaths)—such a burning desire is called Mumukshutâ.[1]

[1] *Mumukshutâ*—This is the fourth Sâdhanâ. With this the student becomes fit to make an enquiry into the highest Truth, i.e. Brahman.

[It is now an accepted principle even in the scientific world that a student in search of knowledge should free himself from all his predispositions and keep an unbiased mind ready to receive whatever is true. The four Sâdhanâs here inculcated are nothing but a course of discipline to attain to such a state of mind.]

उक्तसाधनयुक्तेन विचारः पुरुषेण हि ।
कर्तव्यो ज्ञानसिद्ध्यर्थमात्मनः शुभमिच्छता ॥ १० ॥

उक्तसाधनयुक्तेन In possession of the said qualifications (as means to Knowledge) आत्मनः of one's own शुभमिच्छता desiring good पुरुषेण by a person हि only ज्ञानसिद्ध्यर्थं with a view to attaining Knowledge विचारः constant reflection कर्तव्यः should be practised.

10. Only that person who is in possession of the said qualifications (as means to Knowledge) should constantly reflect[1] with a view to attaining Knowledge, desiring his own good.[2]

[1] *Should constantly reflect*—After a person has attained the tranquillity of the mind through Sâdhanâs, he should strive hard to maintain the same by constantly reflecting on the evanescent nature of this world and withal dwelling on the highest Truth till he becomes one with It.

[2] *Good*—The highest good, i.e. liberation from the bondage of ignorance.

नोत्पद्यते विना ज्ञानं विचारेणान्यसाधनैः ।
यथा पदार्थभानं हि प्रकाशेन विना क्वचित् ॥ ११ ॥

विचारेण विना Without an enquiry (into the Truth) अन्यसाधनैः by other means ज्ञानं Knowledge न not उत्पद्यते is produced यथाहि just as क्वचित् anywhere पदार्थभानं knowledge of objects प्रकाशेन विना without light (न उत्पद्यते is not produced).

11. Knowledge is not brought about by any other means[1] than Vichâra, just as an object is nowhere perceived (seen) without the help of light.

[1] *By any other means*—By Karma, Upâsanâ and the like. It is ignorance or Avidyâ which has withheld the light of Knowledge from us. To get at Knowledge, therefore, we have to remove this Avidyâ. But so long as we are engaged in Karma or Upâsanâ, we remain under its sway. It is only when we make an enquiry into the real nature of this Avidyâ that it gradually withdraws and at last vanishes; then alone Knowledge shines.

कोऽहं कथमिदं जातं को वै कर्ताऽस्य विद्यते ।
उपादानं किमस्तीह विचारः सोऽयमीदृशः ॥ १२ ॥

कोऽहम् (अस्मि) Who am I? इदं this (world) कथं how जातं created कः who वै (expletive) अस्य of this कर्ता the creator विद्यते is इह here (in this creation) उपादानं material किम् what अस्ति is सोऽयं विचारः that Vichâra (enquiry) ईदृशः like this (भवति is).

12. Who am I?[1] How is this (world) created? Who is its creator? Of what material is this (world) made? This is the way of that Vichâra[2] (enquiry).

[1] *Who am I?*—We know that we *are*, but we do not know what our *real nature* is. In the waking state we think that we are the body, the physical being, and consequently feel ourselves strong or weak, young or old. At another time, in the dream state, regardless of the physical existence we remain only in a mental state, where we are merely thinking beings and feel only the misery or happiness that our thoughts create for us. Again, in deep sleep, we enter into a state where we cannot find the least trace of any such attribute whereby we can either assert or deny our existence.

We pass through these states almost daily and yet do not know which of them conforms to our real nature. So the question, 'Who am I?' is always with us an unsolved riddle. It is, therefore, necessary to investigate into it.

[2] *This is the way of that Vichâra*—It is said in the preceding Sloka that Knowledge is attainable by no other means but Vichâra or an enquiry into the Truth. Herein is inculcated in detail the method of such an enquiry.

नाहं भूतगणो देहो नाहं चाक्षगणस्तथा ।
एतद्विलक्षणः कश्चिद्विचारः सोऽयमीदृशः ॥ १३ ॥

अहं I भूतगणः combination of the elements देहः the (gross) body न not (अस्मि am) तथा च so also अहं I न not अक्षगणः (an aggregate of) the senses (i.e. the subtle body)

(अस्मि am ; अहं I) एतद्विलक्षण: different from these कश्चित् something (अस्मि am) सोऽयं, etc.

13. I am neither the body,[1] a combination of the (five) elements (of matter), nor am I an aggregate of the senses; I am something different from these. This is the way of that Vichâra.

[1] *I am neither the body*—This body has its origin in insentient matter and as such it is devoid of consciousness. If I be the body, I should be unconscious; but by no means am I so. Therefore I cannot be the body.

अज्ञानप्रभवं सर्वं ज्ञानेन प्रविलीयते ।
संकल्पो विविधः कर्ता विचारः सोऽयमीदृशः ॥ १४ ॥

सर्वं Everything अज्ञानप्रभवं produced by ignorance (अस्ति is) ज्ञानेन through Knowledge (तत् that) प्रविलीयते completely disappears विविधः various संकल्पः thought कर्ता creator (भवति is) सोऽयं, etc.

14. Everything is produced by ignorance,[1] and dissolves in the wake of Knowledge. The various thoughts (modifications of Antahkarana) must be the creator.[2] Such is this Vichâra.

[1] *Everything is produced by ignorance*—In reply to the question in Sloka 12 as to the cause of this world it is here said that ignorance is the cause of everything.

Sometimes seeing something coiled up on the road we mistake it for a snake and shrink back out of fear. But afterwards when we discover that it is nothing but a piece of rope, the question arises in the mind as to the cause of the appearance of the snake. On enquiry we find that the cause of it lies nowhere else than in our ignorance of the true nature of the rope. So also the cause of the phenomenal world that we see before us lies in the ignorance or Mâyâ that covers the reality.

[2] *The various thoughts . . . . . the creator*—The only thing that we are directly aware of is our own thoughts. The world that we see before us is what our thoughts have created for us. This is clearly understood when we analyse our experiences in dreams. There the so-called material world is altogether absent, and yet the thoughts alone create a world which is as material as the world now before us. It is, therefore, held that the whole universe is, in the same way, but a creation of our thoughts.

एतयोर्यदुपादानमेकं सूक्ष्मं सदव्ययम् ।
यथैव मृद्घटादीनां विचारः सोऽयमीदृशः ॥ १५ ॥

यथैव Just as घटादीनां of the pot and the like (उपादानं material) मृत् earth (भवति is, तथैव so also) एतयो: of these two यत् which उपादानं material (तत् that) एकं one सूक्ष्मं subtle अव्ययं unchanging सत् Sat (Existence) (अस्ति is) सोऽयं, etc.

15. The material (cause) of these two (i.e. ignorance and thought) is the one[1] (without a second), subtle (not apprehended by the senses) and unchanging Sat (Existence), just as the earth is the material (cause) of the pot and the like. This is the way of that Vichâra.

[1] *One*—Because it does not admit of a second of the same or of a different kind, or of any parts within itself. It is one homogeneous whole.

अहमेकोऽपि सूक्ष्मश्च ज्ञाता साक्षी सदव्ययः ।
तदहं नात्र सन्देहो विचारः सोऽयमीदृशः ॥ १६ ॥

(यस्मात् Because) अहं I अपि also एक: one सूक्ष्म: the subtle च (expletive) ज्ञाता the Knower साक्षी the Witness सत् the Existent अव्यय: the Unchanging (अस्मि am, तस्मात् there-

fore) अहं I तत् " That " (अस्मि am) अत्र here सन्देहः doubt
न not (अस्ति is) सोऽयं, etc.

16. As I am also the One, the Subtle, the
Knower,[1] the Witness, the Ever-Existent and the
Unchanging, so there is no doubt that I am
"That"[2] (i.e. Brahman). Such is this enquiry.

[1] *The Knower*—The supreme Knower who is ever present
in all our perceptions as consciousness, and who perceives
even the ego.

When I say, "I know that I exist," the "I" of the
clause 'that I exist' forms a part of the predicate and as
such it cannot be the same 'I' which is the subject. This
predicative 'I' is the ego, the object. The subjective 'I' is
the supreme Knower.

[2] *I am "That"*—I, the ego, when stripped of all its
limiting adjuncts, such as the body and the like, becomes one
with "That," the supreme Ego, i.e. Brahman. In fact, it is
always Brahman ; Its limitation being but the creation of
ignorance.

आत्मा विनिष्कलो ह्येको देहो बहुभिरावृतः ।
तयोरैक्यं प्रपश्यन्ति किमज्ञानमतः परम् ॥ १७ ॥

आत्मा Âtman हि verily एकः one विनिष्कल: without parts
(अस्ति is) देह: the body बहुभि: by many (parts) आवृत:
covered (भवति is. मूढा: the ignorant) तयो: of these two ऐक्यं
identity प्रपश्यन्ति see (confound) अत:परम् else than this किम्
what अज्ञानं ignorance (अस्ति is).

17. Âtman is verily one and without parts,
whereas the body consists of many parts; and
yet the people see (confound) these two as one !
What else can be called ignorance but this ?[1]

¹ *What else can be called ignorance but this?*—To give rise to confusion in knowledge is a unique characteristic of ignorance. It is through the influence of ignorance that one confounds a rope with a snake, a mother-of-pearl with a piece of silver and so on. But, after all, the power of ignorance is not completely manifest there ; for one could easily find an excuse for such confusions when there exist some common characteristics between the real and the apparent. The nature of ignorance is, however, fully revealed when one confounds the subject (i.e. Âtman) with the object (i.e. the body), which have nothing in common between them, being opposed to each other in all respects.

आत्मा नियामकश्चान्तर्देहो बाह्यो नियम्यकः ।
तयोरैक्यं प्रपश्यन्ति किमज्ञानमतः परम् ॥ १८ ॥

आत्मा Âtman नियामकः the ruler अन्तः internal च and (भवति is) देहः the body नियम्यकः the ruled वाह्यः external (भवति is) तयोरैक्यं, etc.

18. Âtman is the ruler of the body and internal, the body is the ruled and external; and yet, etc.

आत्मा ज्ञानमयः पुण्यो देहो मांसमयोऽशुचिः ।
तयोरैक्यं प्रपश्यन्ति किमज्ञानमतः परम् ॥ १९ ॥

आत्मा Âtman ज्ञानमयः all consciousness पुण्यः holy (भवति is) देहः the body मांसमयः all flesh अशुचिः impure (भवति is) तयोरैक्यं, etc.

19. Âtman is all consciousness and holy, the body is all flesh and impure; and yet, etc.

आत्मा प्रकाशकः स्वच्छो देहस्तामस उच्यते ।
तयोरैक्यं प्रपश्यन्ति किमज्ञानमतः परम् ॥ २० ॥

आत्मा Âtman प्रकाशकः the Illuminator स्वच्छः pure देहः the body तामसः of the nature of darkness उच्यते is said तयोरैक्यं, etc.

20. Âtman is the (supreme) Illuminator and purity itself; the body is said to be of the nature of darkness; and yet, etc.

आत्मा नित्यो हि सद्रूपो देहोऽनित्यो ह्यसन्मयः ।
तयोरैक्यं प्रपश्यन्ति किमज्ञानमतः परम् ॥ २१ ॥

आत्मा Âtman नित्यः eternal हि since सद्रूपः Existence itself देहः the body अनित्यः transient हि because असन्मयः non-existence in essence तयोरैक्यं, etc.

21. Âtman is eternal, since it is Existence itself: the body is transient, as it is non-existence in essence;[1] and yet, etc.

[1] *The body is.............non-existence in essence*—The body is undergoing change at every moment, and as such, cannot be eternal. But granting that it is non-eternal, how can it be non-existent?—for, so long as it lasts we surely see it as existing.

At first sight the body appears to be existing, however temporary its existence may be. A relative existence (Vyavahârika Sattâ) is, therefore ascribed to it. But when one examines it and tries to find out its real nature, this so-called tangible body gradually becomes attenuated and at last disappears altogether. It is, therefore, said here that the body, as such, is always non-existent, even though it may appear as existing for a time to those who do not care to see it through.

आत्मनस्तत्प्रकाशत्वं यत्पदार्थावभासनम् ।
नाग्न्यादिदीप्तिवद्दीप्तिर्भवत्यन्यं यतो निशि ॥ २२ ॥

यत् Which पदार्थावभासनं manifestation of all objects तत् that आत्मनः of Âtman प्रकाशत्वं illumination न not अग्न्यादि-

दीप्तिवत् like the light of fire and the rest (आत्मन: of Âtman)
दीप्ति: light (भवति is) यत: for निशि at night आन्ध्यं darkness
भवति exists.

22. The luminosity of Âtman consists in
the manifestation of all objects. Its luminosity
is not[1] like that of fire or any such thing, for
(in spite of the presence of such lights) darkness
prevails at night (at some place or other).

[1] *Its luminosity is not, etc.*—The light of Âtman is unlike any other light. Ordinary lights are opposed to darkness and are limited in their capacity to illumine things.
It is a common experience that where there is darkness there
is no light ; and darkness always prevails at some place or
other, thus limiting the power of illumination of such lights.
Even the light of the sun is unable to dispel darkness at some
places. But the light of Âtman is ever present at all places.
It illumines everything and is opposed to nothing, not even
to darkness; for it is in and through the light of Âtman,
which is present in everybody as consciousness, that one
comprehends darkness as well as light and all other things.

देहोऽहमित्ययं मूढो धृत्वा तिष्ठत्यहो जनः ।
ममायमित्यपि ज्ञात्वा घटद्रष्टेव सर्वदा ॥ २३ ॥

अहो Alas मूढ: ignorant जन: person घटद्रष्टेव like a person
seeing a pot ममायमिति that this is mine सर्वदा ever ज्ञात्वा
knowing अपि even अहं I अयं this देह: body इति that धृत्वा
holding (the view) तिष्ठति rests (contented).

23. How strange is it that a person igno-
rantly rests contented with the idea that he is the
body,[1] while he knows it as something belonging
to him (and therefore apart from him) even as a
person who sees a pot (knows it as apart from
him) !

[1] *The idea that he is the body*—This is the view of Laukâyatikas (Indian materialists) who maintain that man is no more than a fortuitous concourse of material elements. According to them the five elements of matter, through permutations and combinations, have given birth to this body as well as to life and consciousness, and with death everything will dissolve into matter again.

ब्रह्मैवाहं समः शान्तः सच्चिदानंदलक्षणः ।
नाहं देहो ह्यसद्रूपो ज्ञानमित्युच्यते बुधैः ॥ २४ ॥

अहं I ब्रह्म Brahman एव verily (अस्मि am यतः because अहं I) समः equanimous शान्तः quiescent सच्चिदानंदलक्षणः by nature absolute Existence, Knowledge and Bliss (अस्मि am) अहं I असद्रूपः non-existence itself देहः the body नहि never (अस्मि am) इति this बुधैः by the wise ज्ञानम् (true) Knowledge उच्यते is called.

24. I am verily Brahman,[1] being equanimous, quiescent and by nature absolute Existence, Knowledge and Bliss. I am not the body[2] which is non-existence itself. This is called true Knowledge by the wise.

[1] *I am verily Brahman*—'I,' the Self or Âtman, is Brahman, as there is not even a single characteristic differentiating the two. In other words, there are no two entities as Âtman and Brahman ; it is the same entity Âtman that is sometimes called Brahman.

When a person makes an enquiry into the real nature of this external world he is led to one ultimate reality which he calls Brahman. But an enquiry into the nature of the enquirer himself reveals the fact that there is nothing but the Âtman, the Self, wherefrom the so-called external world has emanated. Thus he realizes that what he so long called Brahman, the substratum of the universe, is but his own

Self, it is he himself. So it is said: ' All this is verily Brahman, this Âtman is Brahman ' (*Mând. Up.* 2).

² *I am not the body*—I am neither the gross, subtle nor the causal body.

निर्विकारो निराकारो निरवद्योऽहमव्ययः ।
नाहं देहो ह्यसद्रूपो ज्ञानमित्युच्यते बुधैः ॥ २५ ॥

अहं I निर्विकार: without any change निराकार: without any form निरवद्य: free from all blemishes अव्यय: undecaying (अस्मि am) अहम्, etc.

25. I am without any change, without any form, free from all blemish and decay. I am not, etc.

निरामयो निराभासो निर्विकल्पोऽहमाततः ।
नाहं देहो ह्यसद्रूपो ज्ञानमित्युच्यते बुधैः ॥ २६ ॥

अहं I निरामय: not subject to any disease निराभास: beyond all comprehension निर्विकल्प: free from all alteration आतत: all-pervading (अस्मि am) अहम्, etc.

26. I am not subject to any disease, I am beyond all comprehension,¹ free from all alternatives and all-pervading. I am not, etc.

¹ *I am beyond all comprehension*—I am not comprehended by any thought, for in the supreme Âtman no thought, the thought of the subject and the object, the knower and the known, not even the thought of the Self and the not-Self, is possible, as all thought implies duality whereas the Âtman is non-dual.

निर्गुणो निष्क्रियो नित्यो नित्यमुक्तोऽहमच्युतः ।
नाहं देहो ह्यसद्रूपो ज्ञानमित्युच्यते बुधैः ॥ २७ ॥

अहं I निर्गुण: without any attribute निष्क्रिय: without any activity नित्य: eternal नित्यमुक्त: ever free अच्युत: imperishable (अस्मि am) अहम्, etc.

27. I am without any attribute or activity, I am eternal, ever free and imperishable. I am not, etc.

निर्मलो निश्चलोऽनन्तः शुद्धोऽहमजरोऽमरः ।
नाहं देहो ह्यसद्रूपो ज्ञानमित्युच्यते बुधैः ॥ २८ ॥

अहं I निर्मल: free from all impurity निश्चल: immovable अनन्त: unlimited शुद्ध: holy अजर: undecaying अमर: immortal अहम्, etc.

28. I am free from all impurity, I am immovable, unlimited, holy, undecaying and immortal. I am not, etc.

स्वदेहे शोभनं सन्तं पुरुषाख्यं च संमतम् ।
किं मूर्ख शून्यमात्मानं देहातीतं करोषि भोः ॥ २९ ॥

भो मूर्ख O you ignorant one स्वदेहे (अवस्थितं residing) in your own body देहातीतं beyond the body शोभनं blissful पुरुषाख्यं known as Purusha च (expletive) संमतम् established (by the Sruti as identical with Brahman) सन्तं ever-existent आत्मानं Âtman किं why शून्यं करोषि assert as absolutely non-existent ?

29. O you ignorant one! Why do you assert the blissful, ever-existent Âtman, which resides in your own body and is (evidently) different from it, which is known as Purusha and is established (by the Sruti as identical with Brahman), to be absolutely non-existent[1]?

¹ *Why do you assert............absolutely non-existent?*—
In the preceding stanzas when all the attributes that the
human mind can conceive of have been denied of Âtman, one
is naturally assailed by the doubt whether such an Âtman at
all exists. . To remove this doubt it is here said that Âtman
is a fact of everybody's experience and as such, its existence
cannot be challenged; therefore there is no reason to call it
Sunya or absolute non-existence.

स्वात्मानं श्रृणु मूर्ख त्वं श्रुत्या युक्त्या च पुरुषम् ।
देहातीतं सदाकारं सुदुर्दर्शं भवादृशैः ॥ ३० ॥

(भो:) मूर्ख O you ignorant one त्वं you स्वात्मानं your own
Self श्रुत्या with the help of Sruti युक्त्या by reasoning च also
पुरुषं Purusha देहातीतं beyond the body सदाकारं the very form
of existence (किन्तु but) भवादृशः by persons like you सुदुर्दर्शं
very difficult to be seen श्रृणु (अवधारय) realize.

30. O you ignorant one !   Try to know,
with the help of Sruti¹ and reasoning, your own
Self, Purusha, which is different from the body,
(not a void but) the very form of existence, and
very difficult for persons like you² to realize.

¹ *With the help of Sruti*—With the help of such Sruti
texts as, " Subtler than this Âtman (i.e. the body) which is
full of flesh and blood, there is another Âtman " (*Taitt. Up.*
ii.2). It is thus clearly stated that the Âtman which is sometimes mistaken for the body is, in fact, quite different from it.

² *Persons like you*—Persons of your cast of mind who,
on account of their great attachment to the body, overlook
the vital differences which exist between the body and the
Âtman and blindly assert their identity.

अहंशब्देन विख्यात एक एव स्थितः परः ।
स्थूलस्त्वनेकतां प्राप्तः कथं स्यादेहकः पुमान् ॥ ३१ ॥

पर: Beyond the body (पुरुष: Purusha) अहंशब्देन by the word 'I' विख्यात: known एक एव as only one स्थित: existing (अस्ति is) स्थूल: the gross (body) तु on the other hand अनेकतां manifoldness प्राप्त: obtained (तदा so) देहक: the body कथं how पुमान् Purusha स्यात् can be ?

31. The Supreme (Purusha) known as "I" (ego) is but one, whereas the gross bodies are many. So how can this body be Purusha ?

अहं द्रष्टृतया सिद्धो देहो दृश्यतया स्थितः ।
ममायमिति निर्देशात् कथं स्याद्देहकः पुमान् ॥ ३२ ॥

अहं I द्रष्टृतया as the subject of perception सिद्ध: established (अस्मि am) देह: the body दृश्यतया as the object of perception स्थित: exists अयम् this मम (is) mine इति निर्देशात् on account of this description देहक:, etc.

32. 'I' (ego) is well established as the subject of perception whereas the body is the object. This is learnt from the fact that when we speak of the body we say, 'This is mine.'[1] So how can this body be Purusha ?

[1] *This is mine*—That is, the body is something which I possess, and therefore external to me. So there is not the least chance of its being identified with me (i.e. Ātman).

अहं विकारहीनस्तु देहो नित्यं विकारवान् ।
इति प्रतीयते साक्षात् कथं स्याद्देहकः पुमान् ॥ ३३ ॥

अहं I विकारहीन: without any change (अस्मि am) देह: the body तु but नित्यं ever विकारवान् undergoing changes इति this साक्षात् directly प्रतीयते is perceived देहक:, etc.

33.   It is a fact of direct experience that the
'I' (Âtman) is without any change,[1] whereas the
body is always undergoing changes.   So how
can this body be Purusha ?

[1] *The 'I' (Âtman) is without any change*—In happiness
or misery, in childhood, youth or old age, Âtman, in spite
of many changes in the body, remains the same ; else how
do we recognize a person to be the same man again and
again even though his body and mind have undergone a
thorough change?

यस्मात् परमिति श्रुत्या तया पुरुषलक्षणम् ।
विनिर्णीतं विमूढेन कथं स्यादेहकः पुमान् ॥ ३४ ॥

विमूढेन (विगतो मूढभावो यस्मात्, तेन) By the wise "यस्मात्
परम्" "(There is nothing) higher than He" etc. इति this तया
श्रुत्या by that Sruti text पुरुषलक्षणं the nature of the Purusha
विनिर्णीतं is ascertained देहकः, etc.

34.   Wise men have ascertained the (real)
nature of Purusha from that Sruti text,[1] "(There
is nothing) higher than He (Purusha)," etc.   So
how can this body be Purusha ?

[1] *From that Sruti text*—The text occurs in the Swetâ-
swatara Upanishad (iii, 9) as follows:
" There is nothing higher, subtler or greater than this
Purusha, who stands in the luminous sphere supremely unique
and immovable like a tree, and by whom all this (creation)
is filled."

सर्वं पुरुष एवेति सूक्ते पुरुषसंज्ञिते ।
अप्युच्यते यतः श्रुत्या कथं स्यादेहकः पुमान् ॥ ३५ ॥

यतः Because श्रुत्या by the Sruti पुरुषसंज्ञिते सूक्ते in the
pithy text known as the Purusha Sukta अपि also "पुरुष एव

(इदं) सर्वं" "All this is verily the Purusha" इति thus उच्यते is declared (ततः so) देहकः, etc.

35. Again the Sruti has declared in the Purusha Sukta[1] that "All this is verily the Purusha." So how can this body be Purusha?

[1] *The Purusha Sukta*—It forms a part of the Rig-Veda. There we find one of the highest conceptions of the Cosmic Being wherefrom this universe has emanated. The text here referred to is this:

"The Purusha is verily all this (manifested world). He is all that was in the past and that will be in the future. He is the Lord of the Abode of Bliss and has taken this transient form of the manifested universe, so that the Jivas may undergo the effects of their actions" (*Rig-Veda* X.90.ii).

असङ्गः पुरुषः प्रोक्तो बृहदारण्यकेऽपि च ।
अनन्तमलसंश्लिष्टः कथं स्याद्देहकः पुमान् ॥ ३६ ॥

अपि च So also बृहदारण्यके in the Brihadâranyaka Upanishad पुरुषः Purusha असङ्गः unattached प्रोक्तः is said (ततः so) अनन्तमलसंश्लिष्टः besmeared with innumerable impurities देहकः, etc.

36. So also it is said in the Brihadâranyaka that "The Purusha is completely unattached."[1] How can this body wherein inhere innumerable impurities be the Purusha?

[1] *The Purusha is completely unattache*d—This reference is to the following passages, "The Purusha is not accompanied in the waking state by what he sees in dream, for he is completely unattached to everything" (*Brih. Up.* iv.3. 15-16).

तत्रैव च समाख्यातः स्वयंज्योतिर्हि पुरुषः ।
जडः परप्रकाश्योऽयं कथं स्याद्देहकः पुमान् ॥ ३७ ॥

तत्रैव च There again पुरुष: the Purusha स्वयंज्योति: self-illumined हि (expletive) समाख्यात: is clearly stated (तत: so) अयं this जड: inert परप्रकाश्य: illumined by an external agent देहक:, etc.

37. There again[1] it is clearly stated that "the Purusha is self-illumined." So how can the body which is inert (insentient) and illumined by an external agent be the Purusha ?

[1] *There again*—In the same Brihadâranyaka we have: "Here (in dream) the Purusha is self-illumined" (*Brih. Up.* iv.3.7).

प्रोक्तोऽपि कर्मकाण्डेन ह्यात्मा देहाद्विलक्षणः ।
नित्यश्च तत्फलं भुंक्ते देहपातादनन्तरम् ॥ ३८ ॥

हि Since कर्मकाण्डेन by the Karma-kânda अपि also आत्मा Âtman देहात् from the body विलक्षण: different नित्य: permanent च and प्रोक्त: is declared (यत: as) देहपातादनन्तरं after the fall of the body तत्फलं the results of actions भुंक्ते undergoes.

38. Moreover, the Karma-kânda also declares[1] that the Âtman is different from the body and permanent, as it endures even after the fall of the body and reaps the fruits of actions (done in this life).

[1] *Moreover the Karma-kânda declares*—The Karma-kânda is that portion of the Veda which inculcates the performance of religious acts, sacrifices and ceremonies, laying down in detail rules and regulations for the guidance of its votaries. The followers of the Karma-kânda do not believe in an Iswara or God. Nevertheless they believe in a permanent individual soul which is quite different from the body and which survives the destruction of the latter as a support of Apurva (the abiding result of Karma).

So not only the Jnâna-kânda (the Upanishads) but the Karma-kânda also asserts that Âtman is different from the body.

लिंगं चानेकसंयुक्तं चलं दृश्यं विकारि च ।
अव्यापकमसद्रूपं तत् कथं स्यात् पुमानयम् ॥ ३९ ॥

लिंगं The subtle body च even अनेकसंयुक्तं consisting of many parts चलं unstable दृश्यं an object of perception विकारि changeable च and अव्यापकं limited असद्रूपं non-existent by nature तत् so कथं how अयं this (subtle body) पुमान् Purusha स्यात् can be ?

39. Even the subtle body[1] consists of many parts and is unstable. It is also an object of perception, is changeable, limited and non-existent by nature. So how can this be the Purusha ?

[1] *The subtle body, etc.*—It consists of seventeen parts, viz. the intellect, mind, five organs of perception, five organs of action and five vital forces (or five subtle elements).

एवं देहद्वयादन्य आत्मा पुरुष ईश्वरः ।
सर्वात्मा सर्वरूपश्च सर्वातीतोऽहमव्ययः ॥ ४० ॥

एवं Thus आत्मा Âtman देहद्वयात् from these two bodies अन्यः different अहम् (the substratum of) 'I' (the ego) अव्ययः immutable पुरुषः Purusha ईश्वरः Iswara सर्वात्मा the Self of all सर्वरूपः having all forms सर्वातीतः transcending everything च and.

40. The immutable Âtman, the substratum of the ego, is thus different from these two bodies, and is the Purusha, the Iswara (the Lord of all), the Self of all; It is present in every form and yet transcends them all.

इत्यात्मदेहभागेन प्रपञ्चस्यैव सत्यता ।
यथोक्ता तर्कशास्त्रेण ततः किं पुरुषार्थता ॥ ४१ ॥

इति Thus आत्मदेहभागेन by (enunciating) the difference between the Âtman and the body प्रपञ्चस्यैव सत्यता indeed the reality of the phenomenal world यथा as तर्कशास्त्रेण by Tarka-sâstra उक्ता is said, (तथा in the same way उक्ता is ascertained) ततः so किं पुरुषार्थता (सिध्यति) what ends of human life are served ?

41. Thus the enunciation of the difference between the Âtman and the body has (indirectly) asserted, indeed, after the manner of the Tarka-sâstra,[1] the reality of the phenomenal world. But what ends of human life are served[2] thereby ?

[1] *Tarkasâstra*—The science of logic (Nyâya), or treatises like Sânkhya and Yoga and those of the Laukâyatikas which mostly follow the method of inference in arriving at their respective conclusions. Here it specially refers to Sânkhya which with the mere help of Tarka (logic) tries to establish the final duality of Prakriti and Purusha and in which Prakriti or the material principle that constitutes the phenomenal world is eternal and co-existent with Purusha, the conscious principle.

[2] *What ends of human life are served*—There are generally four ends of human life, viz. Dharma or performance of duty, Artha or attainment of worldly prosperity, Kama or satisfaction of desires, and Moksha or final liberation from the bondage of ignorance, of which the first three are but secondary, as they are only helps to the last which is the *summum bonum*. But this last one, the liberation from the bondage of ignorance, will never be attained unless a person realizes non-duality and becomes one with it, and thus removes even the last vestige of duality from the mind. But the establishment of duality is only an obstacle to such realization and drives persons away from the path of liberation. It, therefore, serves no real purpose in human life.

[But the object of showing the difference between Âtman and the body is not to prove the reality of the body and thus establish the duality of Âman and the body, but only to meet the opponents who hold the view that this body is Âtman. It will be shown in the following stanzas that there is no such thing as body, it is Âtman that alone exists.]

इत्यात्मदेहभेदेन देहात्मत्वं निवारितं ।

इदानीं देहभेदस्य ह्यसत्त्वं स्फुटमुच्यते ॥ ४२ ॥

इति Thus आत्मदेहभेदेन by (the enunciation of) the difference between the Âtman and the body देहात्मत्वं the view that the body is the Âtman निवारितं denied इदानीं now देहभेदस्य the difference between the body and the Âtman हि (expletive) असत्त्वं unreality स्फुटम् clearly उच्यते is stated.

42.   Thus the view that the body is the Âtman has been denounced by the enunciation of the difference between the Âtman and the body. Now is clearly stated the unreality of the difference[1] between the two.

[1] *The unreality of the difference, etc.*—That, the body has no existence independent of the Âtman just as the waves do not exist independently of water. In fact, the Âtman alone exists, and it is through ignorance that one sees it as appearing in the forms of the body and the like.

चैतन्यस्यैकरूपत्वाद्भेदो युक्तो न कर्हिचित् ।

जीवत्वं च मृषा ज्ञेयं रज्जौ सर्पग्रहो यथा ॥ ४३ ॥

चैतन्यस्य Of Consciousness एकरूपत्वात् on account of uniformity कर्हिचित् at any time भेद: division न not युक्त: admissible (भवति is) ; यथा just as रज्जौ in the rope सर्पग्रह: perception of a snake (मृषा false, तथा so) जीवत्वं the individuality of the jiva च also मृषा false ज्ञेयं must be known.

43. No division in Consciousness is admissible at any time as it is always one and the same.[1] Even the individuality of the Jiva must be known as false, like the delusion of a snake in a rope.

[1] *It is always one and the same*—The contents of consciousness may vary, but consciousness as such remains always uniform, just as the light of the sun remains the same while illuminating various objects.

रज्ज्वज्ञानात् क्षणेनैव यद्वद्रज्जुर्हि सर्पिणी ।
भाति तद्वच्चितिः साक्षाद्विश्वाकारेण केवला ॥ ४४ ॥

यद्वत् Just as रज्ज्वज्ञानात् through the ignorance of the rope रज्जुर्हि the very rope क्षणेनैव in an instant सर्पिणी a (female) snake भाति appears तद्वत् in the same way केवला pure चितिः Consciousness साक्षात् without undergoing any change विश्वाकारेण in the form of the phenomenal universe (भाति appears).

44. As through the ignorance of the real nature of the rope the very rope appears in an instant as a snake, so also does pure Consciousness appear in the form of the phenomenal universe without undergoing any change.[1]

[1] *Without undergoing any change*—When a rope appears as a snake nobody can say that any change has been wrought upon the rope. Similarly, pure Consciousness appears as the so-called material universe without undergoing any change whatsoever.

उपादानं प्रपञ्चस्य ब्रह्मणोऽन्यन्न विद्यते ।
तस्मात् सर्वप्रपञ्चोऽयं ब्रह्मैवास्ति न चेतरत् ॥ ४५ ॥

प्रपञ्चस्य Of the phenomenal universe ब्रह्मणः अन्यत् other than Brahman उपादानं material (cause) न not विद्यते is तस्मात्

therefore अयं this सर्वप्रपञ्च: entire phenomenal universe ब्रह्मैव Brahman alone अस्ति is नच not इतरत् anything else.

45. There exists no other material cause of this phenomenal universe except Brahman. Hence this whole universe is but Brahman[1] and nothing else.

[1] *This whole universe is but Brahman*—because the effect is never different from the cause; a pot is never different from the earth of which it is made. The names and forms that differentiate the effect from the cause are but conventional and are found non-existent when their nature is enquired into.

व्याप्यव्यापकता मिथ्या सर्वमात्मेति शासनात् ।

इति ज्ञाते परे तत्त्वे भेदस्यावसरः कुतः ॥ ४६ ॥

सर्वं Everything आत्मा Âtman इति शासनात् from such declaration ·(of the Sruti) व्याप्यव्यापकता the idea of the pervaded and the pervading मिथ्या false (भवति is) इति this परे the supreme तत्त्वे truth ज्ञाते (सति) being realized कुतः where भेदस्य of distinction अवसर: room (अस्ति is).

46. From such declaration[1] (of the Sruti) as "All this is Âtman," it follows that the idea of the pervaded and the pervading is illusory. This supreme truth being realized, where is the room for any distinction between the cause and the effect?

[1] *From such declaration*—It refers to the passage: "These Brahmins and Kshatriyas, these Lokas (regions), gods, Vedas and beings, in short, everything is this Âtman " (*Brih. Up.* iv.57).

श्रुत्या निवारितं नूनं नानात्वं स्वमुखेन हि ।

कथं भासो भवेदन्यः स्थिते चाद्वयकारणे ॥ ४७ ॥

नूनं Certainly खसुखेन हि directly श्रुत्या by the Sruti नानात्वं
manifoldness निवारितं is denied अद्वयकारणे non-dual cause
स्थिते (सति) remaining established कथं how भासः appearance
अन्यः another भवेत् should be ?

47. Certainly the Sruti has directly[1] denied manifoldness in Brahman. The non-dual cause being an established fact,[2] how could the phenomenal universe be different from It?

[1] *The Sruti has directly, etc.*—The Sruti passage runs as
follows: "After hearing from a competent teacher one
should realize with the help of a pure mind that there is no
manifoldness in this (Brahman)." (*Brih. Up.* iv.4.19).

[2] *The non-dual cause being an established fact, etc.*—
The positing of the non-dual Brahman as the final reality by
the Sruti cuts at the root of all causality; for a cause always
presupposes an effect which it produces and which is evidently
different from it in some respect or other. But when there is
only one, how is it possible for a second thing, an effect to
come into existence? The truth is that the non-dual Brahman
or Âtman never causes anything. It is through ignorance
that one sees this world and thinks of Brahman as its cause.

दोषोऽपि विहितः श्रुत्या मृत्योर्मृत्युं स गच्छति ।
इह पश्यति नानात्वं मायया वञ्चितो नरः ॥ ४८ ॥

(यो) नरः The person मायया by Mâyâ (illusion) वञ्चितः
(सन्) being deceived इह in this नानात्वं variety पश्यति sees सः
he मृत्योः from death मृत्युं to death गच्छति goes (इति thus)
श्रुत्या by the Sruti दोषः blame अपि as well विहितः is pro-
nounced.

48. Moreover the Sruti has condemned (the belief in variety) in the words, "The person who," being deceived by Mâyâ, "sees variety in this (Brahman), goes from death to death."[1]

[1] *Goes from death to death*—i.e. is born and dies again
and again. The reference is to such Sruti texts as: " He who
sees variety in this (*i.e.* Brahman), passes from death to
death." (*Brih. Up.* iv.4.19). In other words, unless a person
realizes the non-dual Âtman which is evidently without birth
and death, there is no escape for him from the cycle of
re-births.

ब्रह्मणः सर्वभूतानि जायन्ते परमात्मनः ।
तस्मादेतानि ब्रह्मैव भवन्तीत्यवधारयेत् ॥ ४६ ॥

(यतः As) ब्रह्मणः from Brahman परमात्मनः from the
supreme Âtman सर्वभूतानि all beings जायन्ते are born तस्मात्
therefore एतानि they ब्रह्म Brahman एव verily भवन्ति are इति
this अवधारयेत् clearly understand.

49. Inasmuch as all beings are born of
Brahman,[1] the supreme Âtman, they must be
understood to be verily Brahman.

[1] *All beings are born of Brahman*—The reference here is
to such Sruti passages as: " That is Brahman wherefrom all
these beings are born," etc. (*Taitt. Up.* iii.1).

ब्रह्मैव सर्वनामानि रूपाणि विविधानि च ।
कर्माण्यपि समग्राणि विभर्तीति श्रुतिर्जगौ ॥ ५० ॥

ब्रह्म Brahman एव verily सर्वनामानि all names विविधानि
various रूपाणि forms च and समग्राणि all कर्माणि actions अपि
also विभर्ति sustains इति this श्रुतिः the Sruti जगौ has sung
(clearly declared).

50. The Sruti has clearly declared that
Brahman alone is the substratum[1] of all varieties
of names, forms and actions.

[1] *Brahman alone is the substratum*—Just as a rope is the
substratum of the illusion of a snake and the like, so Brahman
is the substrartum of all names, forms and actions though

these are but illusory ; for even an illusion requires a substratum for its appearance.

सुवर्णाज्जायमानस्य सुवर्णत्वं च शाश्वतम् ।
ब्रह्मणो जायमानस्य ब्रह्मत्वं च तथा भवेत् ॥ ५१ ॥

(यथा As) सुवर्णात् from gold जायमानस्य of (a thing)
produced सुवर्णत्वं the nature of gold च (expletive) शाश्वतं
permanent तथा च so also ब्रह्मणो from Brahman जायमानस्य of
(a being) born ब्रह्मत्वं the nature of Brahman भवेत् is.

51.   Just as a thing made of gold ever has
the nature of gold, so also a being born of
Brahman has always the nature of Brahman.

स्वल्पमप्यन्तरं कृत्वा जीवात्मपरमात्मनोः ।
यः संतिष्ठति मूढात्मा भयं तस्याभिभाषितम् ॥ ५२ ॥

यः Who मूढात्मा the ignorant one जीवात्मपरमात्मनोः between
the Jivâtman and the Paramâtman स्वल्पम् a little अपि even
अन्तरं distinction कृत्वा making संतिष्ठति rests तस्य his भयं fear
(श्रुत्या by the Sruti) अभिभाषितं is spoken of.

52.   Fear[1] is attributed to the ignorant one
who rests[2] after making even the slightest distinction between the Jivâtman and the Paramâtman.

[1] *Fear*—Fear has its root in duality and imperfection and
can be overcome by him alone who realizes non-duality and
thus attains to perfection. For such a person there is none
to be afraid of and nothing to be gained or lost.

[2] *Who rests, etc.*—The Sruti text runs as follows:
" When he (the ignorant one) makes the slightest difference
in It (Brahman) there is fear for him."   (*Taitt. Up.* ii.7).

यत्राज्ञानाद्द्वैतं तमितरस्तत्र पश्यति ।
आत्मत्वेन यदा सर्वं नेतरस्तत्र चाण्वपि ॥ ५३ ॥

यत्र When अज्ञानात् through ignorance द्वैतं duality भवेत्
appears तत्र then इतर: one (इतरं another) पश्यति sees यदा
when सर्वं all आत्मत्वेन as Âtman (भवेत् is) तत्र then इतर: one
च (expletive) अण्वपि even a bit न not (पश्यति sees).

53. When duality[1] appears through ignorance, one sees another; but when everything
becomes identified with the Âtman, one does not
perceive another even in the least.

[1] *When duality, etc.*—This stanza gives the substance of
the following passage from the Sruti: " For when there is
duality, as it were, one sees another, smells another, etc., but
when everything has become one's own Self, how can one see
another, smell another," etc. (*Brih. Up.* iv.5.15).

यस्मिन् सर्वाणि भूतानि ह्यात्मत्वेन विजानतः ।
न वै तस्य भवेन्मोहो न च शोकोऽद्वितीयतः ॥ ५४ ॥

यस्मिन् When सर्वाणि all भूतानि beings हि (expletive) आत्मत्वेन
as Âtman विजानतः of one who realizes तस्य (तस्मिन्) then
न not वै (expletive) मोह: delusion न not च also शोक: sorrow
(भवेत् arises) अद्वितीयतः in consequence of the absence of
duality.

54. In that state[1] when one realizes all as
identified with the Âtman, there arises neither
delusion nor sorrow, in consequence of the
absence of duality.

[1] *In that state, etc.*—It refers to the following Sruti text:
" When a person realizes all beings to be his very Self, where
is there any delusion or sorrow for such a seer of unity?"
(*Isa. Up.* 7).

अयमात्मा हि ब्रह्मैव सर्वात्मकतया स्थितः ।
इति निर्द्धारितं श्रुत्या बृहदारण्यसंस्थया ॥ ५५ ॥

अयं This सर्वात्मकतया as the Self of all स्थितः existing
आत्मा Âtman हि (expletive) ब्रह्म Brahman एव verily इति this
श्रुत्या by the Sruti बृहदारण्यसंस्थया in the form of the Brihadâranyaka निर्द्धारितं declared.

55. The Sruti[1] in the form of the Brihadâranyaka has declared that this Âtman, which is
the Self of all, is verily Brahman.

[1] *The Sruti, etc.*—The text is: "This Âtman is
Brahman," etc. (*Brih. Up.* ii.5.19).

अनुभूतोऽप्ययं लोको व्यवहारक्षमोऽपि सन् ।

असद्रूपो यथा स्वप्न उत्तरक्षणबाधतः ॥ ५६ ॥

अयं This लोकः world अनुभूतः experienced अपि though
व्यवहारक्षमः fit for all practical purposes अपि though सन् being
यथा as स्वप्नः dream (world) (तथा so) उत्तरक्षणबाधतः in consequence of being contradicted in the next moment असद्रूपः of
the nature of non-existence.

56. This world,[1] though an object of our
daily experience and serving all practical purposes, is, like the dream world, of the nature of
non-existence, inasmuch as it is contradicted the
next moment.

[1] *This world, etc.*—We cannot call a thing Sat (ever-
existent) merely because it is experienced and has some
pragmatic value. In dream we experience things which are
valid so long as the dream lasts. But as soon as we awake,
they disappear as though they never existed. So also the
experiences of our waking state, which are so full of meaning
to us, are negated as soon as we enter into dream or deep
sleep. This world of waking experience, therefore, is also in
the same category of existence as the dream world.

स्वप्नो जागरणेऽलीकः स्वप्नेऽपि जागरो न हि ।
द्वयमेव लये नास्ति लयोऽपि ह्युभयोर्न च ॥ ५७ ॥

जागरणे In waking स्वप्नः dream अलीकः unreal स्वप्ने in dream अपि also जागरः waking न not हि surely (अस्ति is) द्वयः both (i.e. waking and dream) एव verily लये in deep sleep नास्ति do not exist लयः deep sleep अपि also हि verily उभयोः in both न not च also (अस्ति is).

57. The dream[1] (experience) is unreal in waking, whereas the waking (experience) is absent in dream. Both, however, are non-existent in deep sleep which, again, is not experienced in either.

[1] *The dream, etc.*—Here the author illustrates the preceding Sloka by showing the unreality of the three states (Avasthâtraya) on account of their mutual contradiction.

त्रयमेवं भवेन्मिथ्या गुणत्रयविनिर्मितम् ।
अस्य द्रष्टा गुणातीतो नित्यो ह्येकश्चिदात्मकः ॥ ५८ ॥

गुणत्रयविनिर्मितं Created by the three Gunas त्रयं the three states एवं thus मिथ्या unreal भवेत् are अस्य their (i.e. of the three states) द्रष्टा witness गुणातीतः beyond all Gunas नित्यः eternal हि (expletive) एकः one चिदात्मकः of the nature of consciousness (अस्ति is).

58. Thus all the three states are unreal[1] inasmuch as they are the creation of the three Gunas; but their witness[2] (the reality behind them) is, beyond all Gunas, eternal one, and is Consciousness itself.

[1] *The three states are unreal, etc.*—This world of our daily experience, comprising these three states, is produced by

the permutation and combination of the three Gunas (components of Prakriti or the primeval substance, viz. Sattva, Rajas and Tamas). But whatever is a compound must disintegrate and be destroyed. This world being a compound is thus foredoomed to destruction; and so it is unreal, as reality implies indestructibility. Here what has been put forward as a mere proposition in Sloka 56 is conclusively proved, viz. that this world though experienced is unreal.

[2] *Their witness*—When everything in this world is in a state of flux and is changing every moment, what is it that sees these changes? The Vedânta declares that it is Ātman, the conscious principle, that witnesses all these changes, itself ever remaining unchanged and unaffected by the Gunas that work these changes.

यद्वन्मृदि घटभ्रान्तिं शुक्तौ वा रजतस्थितिम् ।
तद्ब्रह्मणि जीवत्वं वीक्ष्माणे न पश्यति ॥ ५९ ॥

यद्वत् Just as मृदि in earth घटभ्रान्तिं the illusion of a jar वा or शुक्तौ in the nacre रजतस्थितिं the presence of silver (एक: one) न not पश्यति sees तद्वत् in the same way वीक्ष्माणे when realized ब्रह्मणि in Brahman जीवत्वं Jivahood (न पश्यति does not see).

59. Just as (after the illusion has gone) one is no more deluded to see a jar in earth or silver in the nacre, so does one no more see[1] Jiva in Brahman when the latter is realized (as one's own Self).

[1] *So does one no more see, etc.*—So long as a person is in ignorance, he thinks himself as a Jiva which has an individuality of its own apart from Brahman. But when with the dawn of real knowledge he realizes himself as one with Brahman, this Jivahood appears to him as nothing but an illusion like the illusion of silver in the nacre.

यथा मृदि घटो नाम कनके कुण्डलाभिधा ।
शुक्तौ हि रजतख्यातिर्जीवशब्दस्तथा परे ॥ ६० ॥

यथा Just as मृदि in earth घट: a jar नाम the name कनके
in gold कुण्डलाभिधा the name ear-ring शुक्तौ in a nacre हि
(expletive) रजतख्याति: the name 'silver' (अस्ति is) तथा so परे
in the supreme (Brahman) जीवशब्द: the word Jiva.

60.   Just as earth is described as a jar, gold
as an ear-ring and a nacre as silver, so is
Brahman described as Jiva.

यथैव व्योम्नि नीलत्वं यथा नीरं मरुस्थले ।
पुरुषत्वं यथा स्थाणौ तद्द्विश्वं चिदात्मनि ॥ ६१ ॥

यथैव Just as व्योम्नि in the sky नीलत्वं blueness यथा as
मरुस्थले in the desert नीरं water यथा as स्थाणौ in a post पुरुषत्वं
human figure तद्वत् so चिदात्मनि in the Âtman which is Consciousness विश्वं the universe (अस्ति is).

61.   Just as blueness in the sky, water in
the mirage and a human figure in a post (are but
illusory), so is the universe in Âtman.[1]

[1] *So is the universe in Âtman*—Not only Jiva, but the
whole universe is an illusion in Âtman. This is illustrated in
various ways in Slokas 61—64.

यथैव शून्ये वेतालो गन्धर्वाणां पुरं यथा ।
यथाकाशे द्विचन्द्रत्वं तद्वत् सत्ये जगत्स्थितिः ॥ ६२ ॥

यथैव Just as शून्ये in empty space वेताल: a ghost यथा as
गन्धर्वाणां पुरं a castle in the air यथा as आकाशे in the sky
द्विचन्द्रत्वं the vision of two moons (सन्ति are) तद्वत् in the
same way सत्ये in the supreme Truth (i.e. in Brahman)
जगत्स्थिति: the existence of the universe.

62. Just as the appearance of a ghost in an empty place, of a castle in the air, and of a second moon in the sky (is illusory), so is the appearance of the universe in Brahman.

यथा तरंगकल्लोलैर्जलमेव स्फुरत्यलम् ।

पात्ररूपेण ताम्रं हि ब्रह्माण्डौघैस्तथात्मता ॥ ६३ ॥

यथा Just as तरंगकल्लोलैः as ripples and waves जलं water एव alone पात्ररूपेण in the form of a vessel ताम्रं copper हि verily अलं surely स्फुरति appears तथा so ब्रह्माण्डौघैः as the whole universe आत्मता Âtmanhood (स्फुरति appears).

63. Just as it is water that appears as ripples and waves, or again it is copper that appears in the form of a vessel, so it is Âtman that appears as the whole universe.

घटनाम्ना यथा पृथ्वी पटनाम्ना हि तंतवः ।

जगन्नाम्ना चिदाभाति ज्ञेयं तत्तद्भावतः ॥ ६४ ॥

यथा Just as पृथ्वी earth घटनाम्ना under the name of a jar तन्तवः threads हि verily पटनाम्ना under the name of a cloth (आभान्ति appear, तथा so) चित् Chit (Âtman) जगन्नाम्ना under the name of the universe आभाति appears तद्भावतः by negating those (names) तत् That (Brahman) ज्ञेयं is to be known.

64. Just as it is earth that appears under the name of a jar, or it is threads that appear under a cloth, so it is Âtman that appears under the name of the universe. This Âtman is to be known[1] by negating the names.

[1] *This Âtman is to be known, etc.*—The knowledge of Âtman means only the removal of names and forms that are superimposed upon It through ignorance.

सर्वोऽपि व्यवहारस्तु ब्रह्मणा क्रियते जनैः ।
अज्ञानान्न विजानन्ति मृदेव हि घटादिकम् ॥ ६५ ॥

जनैः By people सर्वः all अपि also व्यवहारः dealing ब्रह्मणा
in and through Brahman क्रियते is performed तु but
अज्ञानात् through ignorance मृत् earth एव alone हि verily
घटादिकं the jars and other earthenwares (इति this) न not
वजानन्ति know (जनाः persons).

65. People perform all their actions in and
through Brahman, (but on account of ignorance
they are not aware of that), just as through
ignorance[1] persons do not know that jars and
other earthenwares are nothing but earth.

[1] *Just as through ignorance, etc.*—In all our dealings with
various earthenwares we are actually dealing with earth, as by
no manner of means can earth be separated from earthenwares.
So in all our intercourse with the world we are, in fact, dealing with Brahman which is non-separable from the world.

कार्यकारणता नित्यमास्ते घटमृदोर्यथा ।
तथैव श्रुतियुक्तिभ्यां प्रपञ्चब्रह्मणोरिह ॥ ६६ ॥

यथा Just as घटमृदो between a jar and earth कार्यकारणता
the relation of effect and cause नित्यं ever आस्ते exists तथैव
so प्रपञ्चब्रह्मणो between the phenomenal world and Brahman
श्रुतियुक्तिभ्यां on the strength of scriptural texts and reasoning
इह here (सा प्रतिपादिता that is established).

66. Just as there ever exists the relation of
cause and effect between earth and a jar, so does
the same relation[1] exist between Brahman and
the phenomenal world; this has been established

here on the strength of scriptural texts and reasoning.

[1] *So does the same relation, etc.*—The same relation of cause and effect exists between Brahman and the world. But as the effect can never be shown to be separate from the cause, this relation only means their non-difference. The Śruti also declares: " All this is identical with That " (*i.e.* Sat or Brahman) (*Chhānd.* VI.8.7); " All this is verily Brahman " (*Chhānd.* III.14.1).

गृह्यमाणे घटे यद्वन्मृत्तिकाऽयाति वै बलात् ।
वीक्ष्यमाणे प्रपञ्चेऽपि ब्रह्मैवाभाति भासुरम् ॥ ६७ ॥

यद्वत् Just as घटे गृह्यमाणे when a jar is perceived मृत्तिका earth वै (expletive) बलात् perforce आयाति accompanies (तथा so) अपि also प्रपञ्चे वीक्ष्यमाणे when the phenomenal world is seen भासुरं shining ब्रह्मैव Brahman alone आभाति flashes.

67. Just as (the consciousness of) earth forces itself upon our mind while thinking of a jar, so also does (the idea of) ever-shining Brahman flash on us[1] while contemplating on the phenomenal world.

[1] *So also does . . . flash on us, etc.*—In some rare moment, while we think very deeply about the evanescent nature of this world, we become almost intuitively aware of Brahman, the permanent entity behind these changing phenomena, for change necessarily implies something that is unchanging.

सदैवात्मा विशुद्धोऽस्ति ह्यशुद्धो भाति वै सदा ।
यथैव द्विविधा रज्जुर्ज्ञानिनोऽज्ञानिनोऽनिशम् ॥ ६८ ॥

आत्मा Ātman सदैव ever विशुद्ध: pure अस्ति is हि verily व (expletive) सदा always अशुद्ध: impure भाति appears यथैव just as रज्जु: a rope अनिशम् always ज्ञानिन: to a wise man

अज्ञानिन: to an ignorant man द्विविधा in two different ways (भाति appears).

68. Âtman, though ever pure[1] (to a wise man), always appears to be impure (to an ignorant one), just as a rope always appears in two different ways[2] to a knowing person and an ignorant one.

[1] *Pure—i.e.* without any modification such as the body.
[2] *In two different ways*—As a rope and as a snake.

यथैव मृन्मयः कुम्भस्तद्वद्देहोऽपि चिन्मयः ।
आत्मानात्मविभागोऽयं मुधैव क्रियतेऽबुधैः ॥ ६९ ॥

यथैव Just as कुम्भः a jar मृन्मयः made of earth तद्वत् so देहः the body अपि also चिन्मयः all consciousness अबुधैः by the ignorant अयं this आत्मानात्मविभागः the division into the Self and non-Self मुधैव in vain क्रियते is made.

69. Just as a jar is all earth, so also is the body all consciousness. The division, therefore, into the Self and non-Self is made by the ignorant to no purpose.[1]

[1] *The division . . . to no purpose*—The dualists erroneously think that the body and Âtman are two separate entities independent of each other. This, however, does them no good, as it deprives them of the realization of the non-dual Âtman which is the *summum bonum*.

सर्पत्वेन यथा रज्जू रजतत्वेन शुक्तिका ।
विनिर्णीता विमूढेन देहत्वेन तथात्मता ॥ ७० ॥

यथा Just as रज्जुः a rope सर्पत्वेन as a snake शुक्तिका a nacre रजतत्वेन as a piece of silver (कल्पिता is imagined) तथा

so आत्मता the nature of Âtman विमूढेन by an ignorant person देहत्वेन as the body विनिर्णीता is determined.

70. Just as a rope is imagined to be a snake and a nacre to be a piece of silver, so is the Âtman determined to be the body by an ignorant person.[1]

[1] *By an ignorant person*—By a rank materialist who declares the body or matter to be the ultimate reality and denies the existence of the Âtman apart from the body.

[How this erroneous knowledge arises out of a confusion between the real and the apparent is illustrated in stanzas 70-74.]

घटत्वेन यथा पृथ्वी पटत्वेनैव तन्तवः ।
विनिर्णीता विमूढेन देहत्वेन तथात्मता ॥ ७१ ॥

यथा Just as पृथ्वी. earth घटत्वेन as a jar तन्तवः threads पटत्वेन as a cloth एव (expletive) तथा so, etc.

71. Just as earth is thought of as a jar (made of it) and threads as a cloth, so is Âtman, etc.

कनकं कुण्डलत्वेन तरङ्गत्वेन वै जलं ।
विनिर्णीता विमूढेन देहत्वेन तथात्मता ॥ ७२ ॥

कनकं Gold कुण्डलत्वेन as an ear-ring जलं water वै (expletive) तरङ्गत्वेन as waves तथा so, etc.

72. Just as gold is thought of as an ear-ring and water as waves, so is the Âtman, etc.

पुरुषत्वेन वै स्थाणुर्जलत्वेन मरीचिका ।
विनिर्णीता विमूढेन देहत्वेन तथात्मता ॥ ७३ ॥

स्थाणुः The stump of a tree पुरुषत्वेन as a human figure व (expletive) मरीचिका a mirage जलत्वेन as water तथा so, etc.

73. Just as the stump of a tree is mistaken for a human figure and a mirage for water, so is the Âtman, etc.

गृहत्वेनैव काष्ठानि खड्गत्वेनैव लोहता ।
विनिर्णीता विमूढेन देहत्वेन तथात्मता ॥ ७४ ॥

काष्ठानि A quantity of wood गृहत्वेन as a house एव (exple_tive) लोहता iron खड्गत्वेन as a sword एव (expletive) तथा so, etc.

74. Just as a mass of wood work is thought of as a house and iron as a sword, so is the Âtman, etc.

[Stanzas 70 and 73 are illustrative of a set of false knowledge due to an error of judgment, whereas the other three stanzas deal only with imperfect knowledge in which forms are made much of in disregard of substance which is the reality behind them.]

यथा वृक्षविपर्यासो जलाद्भवति कस्यचित् ।
तद्वदात्मनि देहत्वं पश्यत्यज्ञानयोगतः ॥ ७५ ॥

यथा Just as जलात् on account of water कस्यचित् to some one वृक्षविपर्यासः the illusion of a tree भवति arises तद्वत् so (जीवः an individual soul) अज्ञानयोगतः through the touch of ignorance आत्मनि in Âtman देहत्वं the physical form पश्यति sees.

75. Just as one sees the illusion[1] of a tree on account of water, so does a person on account of ignorance see Âtman as the body.

[1] *Illusion, etc.*—The tree is not in the water. It is only a reflection due to water that the person sees.

[How ignorance makes one think of the ever-pure Âtman as appearing in material forms is described in stanzas 75-86 through various illustrations culled from everyday experience.]

पोतेन गच्छतः पुंसः सर्वं भातीव चञ्चलं ।

तद्वदात्मनि देहत्वं पश्यत्यज्ञानयोगतः ॥ ७६ ॥

पोतेन By boat गच्छतः going पुंसः to a person सर्वं every-thing चञ्चलं moving इव as if भाति appears तद्वत् so, etc.

76. Just as to a person going in a boat everything appears to be in motion, so does one, etc.

पीतत्वं हि यथा शुभ्रे दोषाद्भवति कस्यचित् ।

तद्वदात्मनि देहत्वं पश्यत्यज्ञानयोगतः ॥ ७७ ॥

यथा Just as कस्यचित् to one दोषात् owing to a defect शुभ्रे in a white thing पीतत्वं yellowness हि verily भवति appears तद्वत् so, etc.

77. Just as to a person suffering from a defect (jaundice) white things appear as yellow, so does one, etc.

चक्षुर्भ्यां भ्रमशीलाभ्यां सर्वं भाति भ्रमात्मकं ।

तद्वदात्मनि देहत्वं पश्यत्यज्ञानयोगतः ॥ ७८ ॥

भ्रमशीलाभ्यां Apt to see wrongly चक्षुर्भ्यां through eyes सर्व everything भ्रमात्मकं defective भाति appears तद्वत् so, etc.

78. Just as to a person with defective eyes everything appears to be defective, so does one, etc.

अलातं भ्रमणेनैव वर्तुलं भाति सूर्यवत् ।

तद्वदात्मनि देहत्वं पश्यत्यज्ञानयोगतः ॥ ७९ ॥

अलातं A firebrand भ्रमणेनैव through mere rotation सूर्यवत्
like the sun वर्तुलं round भाति appears तद्वत् so, etc.

79. Just as a firebrand, through mere
rotation, appears circular like the sun, so does
one, etc.

महत्त्वे सर्ववस्तूनामणुत्वं ह्यतिदूरतः ।
तद्वदात्मनि देहत्वं पश्यत्यज्ञानयोगतः ॥ ८० ॥

सर्ववस्तूनां Of all things महत्त्वे (अपि) in spite of large-
ness अतिदूरतः owing to great distance अणुत्वं minuteness हि
indeed (भाति appears) तद्वत् so, etc.

80. Just as all things that are really large
appear to be very small owing to great distance,
so does one, etc.

सूक्ष्मत्वे सर्वभावानां स्थूलत्वं चोपनेत्रतः ।
तद्वदात्मनि देहत्वं पश्यत्यज्ञानयोगतः ॥ ८१ ॥

सर्वभावानां Of all objects सूक्ष्मत्वे (अपि) in spite of minute
ness उपनेत्रतः through lenses स्थूलत्वं grossness (भवति appears)
तद्वत् so, etc.

81. Just as all objects that are very small
appear to be large when viewed through lenses,
so does one, etc.

काचभूमौ जलत्वं वा जलभूमौ हि काचता ।
तद्वदात्मनि देहत्वं पश्यत्यज्ञानयोगतः ॥ ८२ ॥

काचभूमौ In a surface of glass जलत्वं the state of water
जलभूमौ in a surface of water वा or हि (expletive) काचता the
state of glass (भाति appears) तद्वत् so, etc.

82. Just as a surface of glass is mistaken for water, or *vice versa,* so does one, etc.

यद्वदग्नौ मणित्वं हि मणौ वा वह्निता पुमान् ।

तद्वदात्मनि देहत्वं पश्यत्यज्ञानयोगतः ॥ ८२ ॥

यद्वत् Just as पुमान् a person अग्नौ in fire मणित्वं the state of being a jewel हि (expletive) वा or मणौ in a jewel वह्निता the state of fire (पश्यति sees) तद्वत् so, etc.

83. Just as a person imagines a jewel in fire or *vice versa,* so does one, etc.

अभ्रेषु सत्सु धावत्सु सोमो धावति भाति वै ।

तद्वदात्मनि देहत्वं पश्यत्यज्ञानयोगतः ॥ ८४ ॥

अभ्रेषु धावत्सु सत्सु While clouds move सोमः the moon वै (expletive) धावति is moving (इति thus) भाति appears तद्वत् so, etc.

84. Just as when clouds move, the moon appears to be in motion, so does one, etc.

यथैव दिग्विपर्यासो मोहाद्भवति कस्यचित् ।

तद्वदात्मनि देहत्वं पश्यत्यज्ञानयोगतः ॥ ८५ ॥

यथैव Just as मोहात् through confusion कस्यचित् of one दिग्विपर्यासः mistake about different directions भवति arises तद्वत् so, etc.

85. Just as a person through confusion loses all distinction between the different points of the compass, so does one, etc.

यथा शशी जले भाति चञ्चलत्वेन कस्यचित् ।

तद्वदात्मनि देहत्वं पश्यत्यज्ञानयोगतः ॥ ८६ ॥

यथा Just as शशी the moon जले in water चञ्चलत्वेन as unsteady कस्यचित् to one भाति appears तद्वत् so, etc.

86. Just as[1] the moon (when reflected) in water appears to one as unsteady, so does one, etc.

[1] *Just as, etc.*—It is the reflection which is unsteady, not the moon.

एवमात्मन्यविद्यातो देहाध्यासो हि जायते ।
स एवात्मपरिज्ञानाल्लीयते च परात्मनि ॥ ८७ ॥

एवं Thus अविद्यातः through ignorance आत्मनि in Âtman देहाध्यासः the delusion of the body हि verily जायते arises स एव that very delusion च again आत्मपरिज्ञानात् through the realization of Âtman परात्मनि in the supreme Âtman लीयते disappears.

87. Thus through ignorance arises in Âtman the delusion of the body,[1] which, again, through Self-realization, disappears in the supreme Âtman.[2]

[1] *The delusion of the body*—The delusion of matter in general. In fact, matter is but a concoction of our mind, and therefore has no real existence.

[2] *Which, again . . . . disappears in the supreme Âtman* —When one realizes that Âtman alone is, and nothing else exists, ignorance with all its effects, such as the delusion of the body and the like, ceases to exist for ever.

सर्वमात्मतया ज्ञातं जगत् स्थावरजङ्गमम् ।
अभावात् सर्वभावानां देहस्य चात्मता कुतः ॥ ८८ ॥

(यदा When) स्थावरजङ्गमं immovable and movable सर्वं whole जगत् the universe आत्मतया as Âtman ज्ञातं (भवति) is known (तदा then) सर्वभावानां of all objects अभावात् in consequence of negation देहस्य of the body च (expletive) कुतः where आत्मता appearance as Âtman?

88. When the whole universe, movable and immovable, is known to be Âtman, and thus the existence of everything else is negated, where is then any room[1] to say that the body is Âtman?

[1] *Where is then any room, etc.*—So long as a person is in ignorance he confounds the body with Âtman. But with the dawn of Knowledge, when everything melts away and only the non-dual Âtman remains, there is hardly any room for one to see the body at all, much less to declare it to be Âtman.

आत्मानं सततं जानन् कालं नय महाद्युते ।
प्रारब्धमखिलं भुञ्जन्नोद्वेगं कर्तुमर्हसि ॥ ८६ ॥

(भोः) महाद्युते O thou of great illumination आत्मानं Âtman सततं ever जानन् contemplating अखिलं all प्रारब्धं the Prârabdha भुंजन् experiencing कालं time नय pass उद्वेगं worry कर्तुं to feel न not अर्हसि deserve.

89. O enlightened one, pass your time always contemplating on Âtman while you are experiencing all the results of Prârabdha;[1] for it ill becomes you[2] to feel distressed.

[1] *Prârabdha*—According to the Karma-theory Prârabdha is that part of our past actions which, through their cumulative force, has given birth to this body.

[2] *It ill becomes you, etc.*—Because one who ever dwells on Âtman is already free and above all sorrows, and though he lives and moves like ordinary mortals, he knows it for certain that none of his acts has any binding force upon him.

[There are two other sets of actions known as Sanchita Karma or those of our past actions which are still reserved to

give birth to future bodies, and Kriyamâna Karma or actions
that are being done in this life.]

उत्पन्नेऽप्यात्मविज्ञाने प्रारब्धं नैव मुञ्चति ।
इति यच्छ्रूयते शास्त्रे तन्निराक्रियतेऽधुना ॥ ९० ॥

आत्मविज्ञाने The knowledge of Âtman उत्पन्ने after the
origination of अपि even प्रारब्धं Prârabdha (जनं a person) न
not मुञ्चति leave एव verily इति thus यत् which शास्त्रे in the
scripture श्रूयते is heard तत् that अधुना now निराक्रियते is being
refuted.

90. The theory one hears of from the scripture,[1] that Prârabdha does not lose its hold[2]
upon one even after the origination of the knowledge of Âtman, is now being refuted.

[1] *From the scripture*—From such scriptural texts as:
" The delay in his case is only so long as he is not released
(from the body), then he will attain to Brahman " (*Chhând.
Up.* VI.14.ii).

[2] *Prârabdha does not lose its hold, etc.*—The Śruti in
many places has declared that even a Jnâni is not free from
the operation of Prârabdha. Śankara has dealt with this
point at length in his commentaries on Chhândogya Up. (VI.
14.ii), Vedânta-Sutras (IV.1.xv), and Gitâ (IV.37). In all
those places he has supported the popular view that Prârabdha
is binding on even the Jnâni. But here as well as in his
Vivekachudamani (453—463) he has boldly asserted the true
Vedântic view without any compromise. He has clearly
shown that to a Jnâni there is no such thing as the body, and
it is meaningless to say that he is any longer under the
influence of Prârabdha, which has no hold upon the bodiless
Âtman. The author brings in his arguments in support of
this view in stanzas 91 and 92.

तत्त्वज्ञानोदयादूर्द्धं प्रारब्धं नैव विद्यते ।
देहादीनामसत्त्वात्तु यथा स्वप्नो विबोधतः ॥ ९१ ॥

तत्त्वज्ञानोदयात् ऊर्ध्वं After the origination of the knowledge of Reality तु (expletive) देहादीनां of the body and the like असत्त्वात् in consequence of non-existence प्रारब्धं Prârabdha न not एव verily विद्यते exists यथा just as खप्न: dream विबोधतः on waking.

91.   After the origination of the knowledge of Reality Prârabdha verily ceases to exist, inasmuch as the body[1] and the like become non-existent; just as a dream does not exist on waking.

[1] *Inasmuch as the body, etc.*—The body, mind, intelligence and the like have their existence only in ignorance and therefore cannot exist when the latter is entirely destroyed by Knowledge. In the absence of the body, Prârabdha also necessarily ceases to exist, since there remains nothing on which it can act.

कर्म जन्मान्तरीयं यत् प्रारब्धमिति कीर्तितम् ।

तत्तु जन्मान्तराभावात् पुंसो नैवास्ति कर्हिचित् ॥ ६२ ॥

जन्मान्तरीयं Acquired in a previous life यत् which कर्म Karma (तत् that) प्रारब्धं Prârabdha इति as कीर्तितं is called पुंस: of the man (of knowledge) जन्मान्तराभावात् in the absence of future birth तत् that (Prârabdha) तु but न not एव verily कर्हिचित् at any time अस्ति exists.

92.   That Karma which is done in a previous life is known as Prârabdha (with respect to this life which it has brought forth). But such a Prârabdha does not exist[1] (for a man of knowledge), as he has no other birth.

स्वप्नदेहो यथाध्यस्तस्तथैवायं हि देहकः ।

अध्यस्तस्य कुतो जन्म जन्माभावे हि तत् कुतः ॥ ६३ ॥

यथा Just as स्वप्नदेहः the body in a dream अध्यस्तः is superimposed तथा so हि (expletive) अयं this देहकः the body (अध्यस्तः is superimposed) एव verily अध्यस्तस्य of what is superimposed जन्म birth कुतः how (सम्भवति is possible) जन्माभावे in the absence of birth (of the body) तत् that (Prârabdha) कुतः how हि at all (अस्ति is) ?

93. Just as the body in a dream is superimposed (and therefore illusory), so is also this body.[1] How could there be any birth of the superimposed (body), and in the absence of birth[2] (of the body) where is the room for that (i.e. Prârabdha) at all?

[1] *So is also this body*—This body of the waking state is also a superimposition on the Âtman and is therefore unreal. Only an ignorant man thinks this body to be more real than the body assumed in a dream, but to a man of knowledge there exists no such distinction, inasmuch as both are but the creation of the mind through ignorance.

[2] *In the absence of birth*—Prârabdha is imagined as the cause of the body, but when there is no such thing as the body, there is hardly any scope for Prârabdha.

उपादानं प्रपञ्चस्य मृद्भाण्डस्येव कथ्यते ।
अज्ञानं चैव वेदान्तैस्तस्मिन्नष्टे क विश्वता ॥ ६४ ॥

वेदान्तैः By the Vedânta texts भाण्डस्य of a jar मृत् earth इव like प्रपञ्चस्य of the phenomenal world अज्ञानं ignorance च (expletive) उपादानं the material (cause) एव verily कथ्यते is declared तस्मिन्नष्टे that being destroyed विश्वता the state of the universe क where (तिष्ठति subsists)?

94. The Vedânta texts declare[1] ignorance to be verily the material (cause) of the

phenomenal world, just as earth is of a jar. That (ignorance) being destroyed,[2] where can the universe subsist?

[1] *The Vedânta texts declare, etc.*—The word Vedânta here means the Upanishads which form the latter part of the Vedas. The texts alluded to here are: " Know Mâyâ (ignorance) to be the Prakriti (i.e. material of the universe) (*Sveta. Up.* iv.10), and so on.

[2] *That (ignorance) being destroyed, etc.*—The cause being completely destroyed, the effect must cease to exist. A piece of cloth cannot exist when the threads are all burnt; so the world cannot continue when ignorance is destroyed.

यथा रज्जुं परित्यज्य सर्पं गृह्णाति वै भ्रमात् ।
तद्वत् सत्यमविज्ञाय जगत् पश्यति मूढधीः ॥ ९५ ॥

यथा Just as (जनः a person) भ्रमात् out of confusion रज्जुं the rope परित्यज्य leaving aside सर्पं the snake वै indeed गृह्णाति perceives तद्वत् so मूढधीः an ignorant person सत्यं truth अविज्ञाय without knowing जगत् the phenomenal world पश्यति sees.

95. Just as a person out of confusion perceives only the snake leaving aside the rope, so does an ignorant person see only the phenomenal world without knowing the reality.

रज्जुरूपे परिज्ञाते सर्पखण्डं न तिष्ठति ।
अधिष्ठाने तथा ज्ञाते प्रपञ्चः शून्यतां गतः ॥ ९६ ॥

रज्जुरूपे (On) the real nature of the rope परिज्ञाते being known सर्पखण्डं the appearance of the snake न not तिष्ठति remains तथा so अधिष्ठाने ज्ञाते the substratum (the reality behind) being known प्रपञ्चः the phenomenal world शून्यतां extinction गतः attains.

96. The real nature of the rope being known, the appearance of the snake no longer persists; so the substratum being known,[1] the phenomenal world disappears completely.

[1] *The substratum being known, etc.*—This illusory world has Brahman as its substratum which is hidden from one's view on account of ignorance. But when one realizes this Brahman by removing ignorance, one is no more deluded into seeing the phenomenal world which, like all other illusory things, vanishes completely before the knowledge of the truth.

देहस्यापि प्रपञ्चत्वात् प्रारब्धावस्थितिः कुतः ।
अज्ञानिजनबोधार्थं प्रारब्धं वक्ति वै श्रुतिः ॥ ९७ ॥

देहस्य Of the body अपि also प्रपञ्चत्वात् on account of phenomenality प्रारब्धावस्थिति: the existence of Prârabdha कुत: how (अस्ति is) श्रुति: the Sruti अज्ञानिजनबोधार्थं for the understanding of the ignorant folk वै only प्रारब्धं Prârabdha वक्ति speaks.

97. The body also being within the phenomenal world (and therefore unreal), how could Prârabdha exist? It is, therefore, for the understanding of the ignorant[1] alone that the Sruti speaks of Prârabdha.

[1] *For the understanding of the ignorant*—Those who do not know the highest truth argue that if ignorance with all its effects is destroyed by Knowledge, how does the body of a Jnâni live, and how is it possible for him to behave like ordinary mortals? They, however, fail to see that it is they who, being still in ignorance, see the body of a Jnâni and speak of him as behaving this way or that, whereas the Jnâni himself never sees the body at all, as he is ever established in Âtman. To convince such persons the Śruti brings

in Prârabdha as a tentative explanation for the so-called behaviour of a Jnâni.

क्षीयन्ते चास्य कर्माणि तस्मिन् दृष्टे परावरे ।
बहुत्वं तन्निषेधार्थं श्रुत्या गीतं च यत् स्फुटम् ॥ ९८ ॥

तस्मिन् परावरे (On) that which is both the higher and the lower दृष्टे being realized अस्य his कर्माणि all actions च and क्षीयन्ते are destroyed (इति thus) श्रुत्या by the Sruti बहुत्वं the use of the plural number यत् which स्फुटं clearly गीतं is declared (तत् that) च also तन्निषेधार्थं for the negation of that (Prârabdha).

98. "And all the actions[1] of a man perish when he realizes that (Âtman) which is both the higher and the lower." Here the clear use of the plural[2] by the Sruti is to negate Prârabdha as well.

[1] "And all the actions," etc.—The Śruti text runs as follows: "The knot of the heart breaks, all doubts vanish and (all) his actions perish when a person realizes that which is both the higher and the lower" (Mund. Up. II.2.viii).

[2] Here . . . the plural, etc.—The Sruti by using the term 'actions' has very clearly declared that not only Sanchita and Kriyamâna Karmas but also Prârabdha Karma is destroyed by knowledge. The Gitâ also declares, "O Arjuna, the fire of knowledge reduces all actions into ashes" (IV.37). Moreover, it also stands to reason that Prârabdha, an effect of ignorance, must cease to exist when the latter is destroyed by knowledge.

उच्यतेऽज्ञैर्बलाच्चैतत्तदानर्थद्वयागमः ।
वेदान्तमतहानं च यतो ज्ञानमिति श्रुतिः ॥ ९९ ॥

अज्ञैः By the ignorant बलात् perforce एतत् this उच्यते is maintained च still तदा then अनर्थद्वयागमः room for two

absurdities (भविष्यति will be) वेदान्तमतहानं abandonment
of the Vedântic conclusion च also (अतः) therefore यतः
from which ज्ञानं knowledge (भवति arises) इति (सा) that
श्रुतिः Sruti (ग्राह्या should be accepted).

99. If the ignorant still arbitrarily[1] maintains this,[2] they will not only involve themselves
into two absurdities[3] but will also run the risk of
forgoing the Vedântic conclusion.[4] So one should
accept those Srutis alone[5] from which proceeds
true knowledge.

[1] *Arbitrarily*—By sheer force of one's own predilections,
and not on the strength of sound reasoning.

[2] *This*—i.e. the possibility of Prârabdha and its action
even after knowledge.

[3] *Involve themselves into two absurdities*—The upholders
of Prârabdha are driven to this absurd position : In the first
place Moksha or liberation from the bonds of duality will be
impossible for them, as there will always remain a second
thing, Prârabdha, along with Brahman; and in the second
place liberation, the sole aim of knowledge, being impossible,
there will hardly remain any utility of knowledge, and in that
case they have to give up the Sruti on which they build their
theory, as useless, since the Sruti has no other function but
to lead to knowledge. Such are the disastrous consequences
one has to encounter if one is to maintain Prârabdha to the
end.

[4] *Run the risk of forgoing the Vedântic conclusion*—The
final conclusion of the Vedânta is that there is only one non-
dual Brahman or Âtman which is birthless, deathless and free
from all modifications. The world of duality is the creation
of ignorance and will cease to exist when the latter is
destroyed by knowledge. So persons who maintain that
Prârabdha will remain even after knowledge and thus uphold
a sort of duality even in the last stage, surely sacrifice the
ultimate Vedântic truth which is essentially non-dual in its
character.

⁵ *Those Srutis alone, etc.*—The realization of the non-dual Âtman alone constitutes the real knowledge, and the Srutis are the only means to such knowledge. But all of them do not bring about this knowledge. So those Srutis alone which teach the non-dual Âtman and thus directly lead us to the final realization, are to be accepted as the real, and all others that support duality are to be treated as secondary, as they have no direct bearing upon the knowledge of Truth.

[In connection with the main topic it may be said that one should abide by those Srutis alone which establish the non-dual Âtman by denying all actions of it, and not by those that maintain Prârabdha and thus lend support to duality].

त्रिपञ्चाङ्गान्यथो वक्ष्ये पूर्वोक्तस्य हि लब्धये ।
तैश्च सर्वैः सदा कार्यं निदिध्यासनमेव तु ॥ १०० ॥

अथो Now पूर्वोक्तस्य of the aforesaid (knowledge) हि (expletive) लब्धये for the attainment त्रिपञ्चाङ्गानि fifteen steps (अहं I) वक्ष्ये shall expound तैः सर्वैः by the help of them all च (expletive) निदिध्यासनम् profound meditation एव verily तु (expletive) सदा always कार्यम् should be practised.

100. Now, for the attainment¹ of the aforesaid (knowledge) I shall expound the fifteen steps by the help of which one should practise profound meditation at all times.

¹ *Now, for the attainment, etc.*—Verses 24-28 have set forth in detail the nature of knowledge which is the goal of life. But it is not sufficient only to know about the goal, one must acquaint oneself with the means of its attainment as well. The fifteen steps here inculcated are the means which, if earnestly followed, will gradually lead the initiate to the desired goal.

नित्याभ्यासादृते प्राप्तिं न भवेत् सच्चिदात्मनः ।
तस्माद् ब्रह्म निदिध्यासेज्जिज्ञासुः श्रेयसे चिरम् ॥ १०१ ॥

निल्याभ्यासाद्दते Without constant practice सचिदात्मनः of the Âtman that is absolute existence and knowledge प्राप्तिः realization न not भवेत् arises तस्मात् so जिज्ञासुः the seeker after knowledge श्रेयसे for the highest good ब्रह्म Brahman चिरं long निदिध्यासेत् should meditate.

101. The Âtman that is absolute existence and knowledge cannot be realized without constant practice. So one seeking after knowledge should long meditate upon Brahman[1] for the attainment of the desired goal.

[1] *Should long meditate upon Brahman*—The realization of Brahman does not come in a day; it requires years of strenuous effort. One should not, therefore, give up one's practice even if one meets with failure in the initial stages, but should continue it with renewed vigour. Sri Ramakrishna used to say: a *bonafide* cultivator never gives up his cultivation even if there is no crop for a few years; he continues it with ever-increasing zeal till he reaps a good harvest. So should a true aspirant.

यमो हि नियमस्त्यागो मौनं देशश्च कालता ।

आसनं मूलबन्धश्च देहसाम्यं च दृक्स्थितिः ॥ १०२ ॥

प्राणसंयमनं चैव प्रत्याहारश्च धारणा ।

आत्मध्यानं समाधिश्च प्रोक्तान्यङ्गानि वै क्रमात् ॥ १०३ ॥

यमः Control of the senses हि (expletive) नियमः control of the mind त्यागः renunciation मौनं silence देशः place कालता time च and आसनं posture मूलबन्धः the root that restrains च and देहसाम्यं equipoise of the body दृक्स्थितिः steadiness of vision च and प्राणसंयमनं control of the vital forces एव also प्रत्याहारः self-withdrawal धारणा concentration च and आत्मध्यानं meditation on Âtman समाधिः complete

absorption च and वै (expletive) अज्ञानि the steps क्रमात्
in order प्रोक्तानि are described.

102-103. The steps,[1] in order, are described
as follows: the control of the senses, the control
of the mind, renunciation, silence, space, time,
posture, the restraining root (Mulabandha), the
equipoise of the body, the firmness of vision, the
control of the vital forces, the withdrawal of the
mind, concentration, self-contemplation, and
complete absorption.

[1] *The steps*—These fifteen steps include the eight steps
of Patanjali, but with a reorientation of meaning as will be
evident from the following.

सर्वं ब्रह्मेति विज्ञानादिन्द्रियग्रामसंयमः ।
यमोऽयमिति संप्रोक्तोऽभ्यसनीयो मुहुर्मुहुः ॥ १०४ ॥

सर्वं All ब्रह्म Brahman (अस्ति is) इति विज्ञानात् from such
knowledge इन्द्रियग्रामसंयमः the restraint of all the senses अयं
this यम इति as Yama संप्रोक्तः is rightly called (सः this) मुहुर्मुहुः
repeatedly अभ्यसनीयः should be practised.

104. The restraint of all the senses by means
of such knowledge as "All this is Brahman" is
rightly called Yama,[1] which should be practised
again and again.

[1] *Yama*—Patanjali describes it as "non-killing, truth-
fulness, non-stealing, continence, and non-receiving" (II.30);
but when one knows everything to be Brahman all of these
follow as a matter of course.

सजातीयप्रवाहश्च विजातीयतिरस्कृतिः ।
नियमो हि परानन्दो नियमात् क्रियते बुधैः ॥ १०५ ॥

सजातीयप्रवाह: The continuous flow of one kind of thought विजातीयतिरस्कृति: the rejection of all that is foreign to it च and (इति this) नियम: Niyama (उच्यते is called) (अयं this) हि verily परानन्द: the supreme bliss (अयं this) बुधै: by the wise नियमात् regularly क्रियते is practised.

105. The continuous flow of only one kind of thought,[1] to the exclusion of all other thoughts, is called Niyama,[2] which is verily the supreme bliss and is regularly practised by the wise.

[1] *One kind of thought*—Thought relating to the unity of the individual self with Brahman such as " This Âtman is Brahman," and " I am Brahman."

[2] *Niyama*—According to Patanjali Niyama is " internal and external purification, contentment, mortification, Vedic study, and worship of God " (II.32). These, however, are easily accessible to one who constantly dwells on Brahman.

त्यागः प्रपञ्चरूपस्य चिदात्मत्वावलोकनात् ।

त्यागो हि महतां पूज्यः सद्यो मोक्षमयो यतः ॥ १०६ ॥

चिदात्मत्वावलोकनात् Realizing it as the all-conscious Âtman प्रपञ्चरूपस्य of the illusory universe त्याग: abandonment हि verily महतां of the great पूज्य: honoured त्याग: renunciation (अस्ति is) यत: because (अयं this) सद्य: immediately मोक्षमय: of the nature of liberation (भवति is).

106. The abandonment of the illusory universe by realizing it as the all-conscious Âtman is the real[1] renunciation honoured by the great, since it is of the nature of immediate liberation.

[1] *The real renunciation*—Some explain renunciation as the giving up of all kinds of actions whether scriptural or mundane, and thus attaining to a state of inactivity. This, however, is far from what is really meant by renunciation

which, in its deepest sense, is all positive. It is when one realizes Âtman everywhere and thus covets nothing, that one is said to have real renunciation. The Sruti also declares, " Clothe everything in this transitory world with God and thus maintain thyself by that renunciation," etc. (*Isâ.* I).

यस्माद्वाचो निवर्तन्ते अप्राप्य मनसा सह ।
यन्मौनं योगिभिर्गम्यं तद्ब्रवेत् सर्वदा बुधः ॥ १०७ ॥

वाचः Words (तत् that) अप्राप्य without reaching मनसा सह with the mind यस्मात् from which निवर्तन्ते turn back यत् which मौनं silence योगिभिः by the Yogins गम्यं attainable बुधः the wise सर्वदा always तत् that भवेत् should be.

107. The wise should always be one with that silence[1] wherefrom words[2] together with the mind turn back without reaching it, but which is attainable by the Yogins.[3]

[1] *That silence*—Here it denotes Âtman which is ever quiescent.

[2] *Wherefrom words, etc.*—It is a reference to the Taittiriya Upanishad (II.9).

[3] *Attainable by the Yogins*—Because it is their very Self.

वाचो यस्मान्निवर्तन्ते तद्वक्तुं केन शक्यते ।
प्रपञ्चो यदि वक्तव्यः सोऽपि शब्दविवर्जितः ॥ १०८ ॥

इति वा तद्ब्रवेन्मौनं सतां सहजसंज्ञितम् ।
गिरा मौनं तु बालानां प्रयुक्तं ब्रह्मवादिभिः ॥ १०९ ॥

यस्मात् From which वाचः words निवर्तन्ते turn back तत् that केन by whom वक्तुं to be described शक्यते is capable यदि if प्रपञ्चः the phenomenal world वक्तव्यः to be spoken of सोऽपि even that शब्दविवर्जितः devoid of words (भवति is) or this इति

वा or this (यत् which) सतां among the sages सहजसंज्ञितं called congenital तत् that मौनं silence भवेत् is गिरा by (restraining) speech मौनं silence ब्रह्मवादिभिः by the teachers of Brahman बालानां for children प्रयुक्तं ordained.

108-109. Who can describe That (i.e. Brahman) whence words turn away? (So silence is inevitable while describing Brahman). Or if the phenomenal world were to be described, even that is beyond words.[1] This,[2] to give an alternate definition, may also be termed silence known among the sages as congenital.[3] The observance of silence by restraining speech, on the other hand, is ordained by the teachers of Brahman for the ignorant.

[1] *Even that is beyond words*—Even this world, when one attempts to describe it, is found to be inexpressible, since it cannot be called either Sat (existent) or Asat (non-existent). If it were Sat it would not disappear in deep sleep, and if Asat, it would not at all appear now. Therefore this world is also Anirvachaniya (inexpressible).

[2] *This*—The inexpressibility of Brahman and the world.

[3] *Congenital*—Inseparable from Âtman.

आदावन्ते च मध्ये च जनो यस्मिन्न विद्यते ।
येनेदं सततं व्याप्तं स देशो विजनः स्मृतः ॥ ११० ॥

आदौ In the beginning अन्ते in the end च and मध्ये in the middle च as also यस्मिन् in which जनः people (i. e. the universe) न not विद्यते exists येन by which इदं this (universe) सततं always व्याप्तं is pervaded सः that विजनः solitude देशः space स्मृतः is known.

110. That solitude[1] is known as space, wherein the universe does not exist in the

beginning, end or middle, but whereby it is pervaded at all times.

[1] *That solitude*—Here it is Brahman that is indicated, for Brahman alone is solitary since It admits of no second at any time.

कलनात् सर्वभूतानां ब्रह्मादीनां निमेषतः ।
कालशब्देन निर्दिष्टो ह्यखण्डानन्दकोऽद्वयः ॥ १११ ॥

निमेषतः In the twinkling of an eye ब्रह्मादीनां beginning with Brahmā सर्वभूतानां of all beings कलनात् on account of producing अखण्डानन्दकः undivided bliss अद्वयः non-dual हि (verily) कालशब्देन by the word time निर्दिष्टः is denoted.

111. The non-dual (Brahman) that is bliss indivisible is denoted by the word 'time,' since it brings into existence,[1] in the twinkling of an eye, all beings from Brahmā downwards.

[1] *It brings into existence, etc.*—The whole creation is nothing but a resolve in the mind of God. When He has a desire for Creation the universe is produced in no time. A parallel case we find in our dream when the whole dream-world is brought into being in an instant by a mere wish.

Not only the power of creation but also that of preservation and destruction is also meant.

सुखेनैव भवेद्यस्मिन्नजस्रं ब्रह्मचिन्तनम् ।
आसनं तद्विजानीयान्नेतरत् सुखनाशनम् ॥ ११२ ॥

यस्मिन् Where सुखेन easily एव verily अजस्रं unceasingly ब्रह्मचिन्तनम् meditation of Brahman भवेत् becomes तत् that आसनम् (इति) to be posture विजानीयात् should know ; सुखनाशनम् destroying happiness इतरत् any other न not.

112. One should know that[1] to be real posture in which the meditation of Brahman

flows spontaneously and unceasingly, and not any other[2] that destroys one's happiness.

[1] *That, etc.*—i.e. a serene state of the constitution.

[2] *Not any other, etc.*—Not any posture which brings about physical pains and thus distracts the mind from the meditation of Brahman by dragging it down to the lower plane.

सिद्धं यत् सर्वभूतादि विश्वाधिष्ठानमव्ययम् ।
यस्मिन् सिद्धाः समाविष्टास्तद्वै सिद्धासनं विदुः ॥ ११३ ॥

यत् Which सर्वभूतादि the origin of all beings विश्वाधिष्ठानम् the support of the whole universe अव्ययम् immutable (इति thus) सिद्धं well known यस्मिन् in which सिद्धाः Siddhas (the enlightened) समाविष्टाः completely absorbed तत् that वै alone (पण्डिताः the wise) सिद्धासनं as Siddhâsana विदुः know.

113. That which is well known as the origin of all beings and the support of the whole universe, which is immutable and in which the enlightened are completely merged—that alone is known as Siddhâsana.[1]

[1] *Siddhâsana*—This is the name of a particular Yogic posture, but here it only means the eternal Brahman.

[Incidentally two particular postures known to the Yogis are mentioned in this and the next verse, and explained with reference to Brahman.]

यन्मूलं सर्वभूतानां यन्मूलं चित्तबन्धनम् ।
मूलबन्धः सदा सेव्यो योग्योऽसौ राजयोगिनाम् ॥ ११४ ॥

यत् Which सर्वभूतानां of all existence मूलं the root चित्तबन्धनम् the restraint of the mind यन्मूलं on which is rooted (तत् that) मूलबन्धः the restraining root (उच्यते is called)

राजयोगिनाम् of the Rāja-yogins योग्य: fit असौ this सदा always
सेव्य: should be adopted.

114. That (Brahman) which is the root of all
existence and on which the restraint of the mind[1]
is based is called the restraining root (Mulabandha)[2] which should always be adopted since
it is fit for Rāja-yogins.

[1] *The restraint of the mind, etc.*—It is through complete
mergence in Brahman that the mind is truly restrained.

[2] *Mulabandha*—This is also the name of another Yogic
posture.

[The truth underlying all this is that while seated for
meditation one should not bother much about the postures,
but always try to engage one's whole attention to the meditation of Brahman which alone constitutes the goal.]

अङ्गानां समतां विद्यात् समे ब्रह्मणि लीनताम् ।
नो चेन्नैव समानत्वमृजुत्वं शुष्कवृक्षवत् ॥ ११५ ॥

समे Homogeneous ब्रह्मणि in Brahman लीनतां absorption
अङ्गानां of the limbs समतां equipoise विद्यात् should know नो चेत्
otherwise शुष्कवृक्षवत् like a dried-up tree ऋजुत्वं straightness
न not एव verily समानत्वम् equipoise (भवति is).

115. Absorption in the uniform Brahman
should be known as the equipoise of the limbs
(Dehasâmya). Otherwise mere straightening of
the body like that of a dried-up tree is no equipoise.

दृष्टिं ज्ञानमयीं कृत्वा पश्येद्ब्रह्ममयं जगत् ।
सा दृष्टिः परमोदारा न नासाग्रावलोकिनी ॥ ११६ ॥

दृष्टिं The vision ज्ञानमयीं full of knowledge कृत्वा making
जगत् the world ब्रह्ममयं to be Brahman itself पश्येत् should view

सा that दृष्टि: vision परमोदारा noble (भवति is) न not नासाग्राव-
लोकिनी that which sees the tip of the nose.

116. Converting the ordinary vision into one
of knowledge one should view the world as
Brahman Itself. That is the noblest vision,[1] and
not that which is directed to the tip of the nose.

[1]*Noblest vision*—Because before it there is no distinction of high or low, great or small, since everything is merged
in one all-pervading Brahman.

द्रष्टृदर्शनदृश्यानां विरामो यत्र वा भवेत् ।
दृष्टिस्तत्रैव कर्तव्या न नासाग्रावलोकिनी ॥ ११७ ॥

वा Or द्रष्टृदर्शनदृश्यानां of the seer, sight and the seen यत्र
where विराम: cessation भवेत् happens तत्रव there alone दृष्टि:
vision कर्तव्या should be directed न not नासाग्रावलोकिनी
seeing the tip of the nose.

117. Or, one should direct one's vision to
That[1] alone where all distinction of the seer, sight
and the seen ceases and not to the tip of the nose.[2]

[1] *To That*—i.e. to Brahman which is pure consciousness,
and wherein alone ceases the distinction of the seer, sight and
the seen, that *a priori* triad of all perceptions.

[2] *Not to the tip of the nose*—It is said that while seated
for meditation one is to gaze on the tip of the nose (*Gitâ*,
VI.13). But one should not take it too literally, as in that
case the mind will think not of Âtman, but of the nose. As
a matter of fact, one is to concentrate one's mind on Âtman
alone, leaving aside all external things. This is why meditation of Âtman is here emphasized and mere gazing on the tip
of the nose is condemned.

चित्तादिसर्वभावेषु ब्रह्मत्वेनैव भावनात् ।
निरोधः सर्ववृत्तीनां प्राणायामः स उच्यते ॥ ११८ ॥

चित्तादिसर्वभावेषु In all mental states such as Chitta ब्रह्मत्वेन as Brahman एव verily भावनात् through the faculty of remembrance सर्ववृत्तीनां of all modifications of the mind (य: which) निरोध: restraint स: that प्राणायाम: Prânâyâma (control of the vital forces) उच्यते is called.

118. The restraint of all modifications of the mind by regarding all mental states like the Chitta as Brahman alone, is called Prânâyâma.

निषेधनं प्रपञ्चस्य रेचकाख्यः समीरणः ।

ब्रह्मैवास्मीति या वृत्तिः पूरको वायुरीरितः ॥ ११९ ॥

ततस्तद्वृत्तिनैश्चल्यं कुंभकः प्राणसंयमः ।

अयं चापि प्रबुद्धानामज्ञानां घ्राणपीडनम् ॥ १२०॥

प्रपञ्चस्य Of the phenomenal world निषेधनं negation रेचकाख्यः known as Rechaka (inhalation) समीरण: breath (अस्ति is) अहं I ब्रह्म Brahman एव alone अस्मि am इति that या which वृत्ति: thought (सा that) पूरक: Puraka (inhalation) वायु: breath ईरित: is called तत: thereafter तद्वृत्तिनैश्चल्यं the steadiness of that thought कुम्भक: Kumbhaka (holding the breath) (उच्यते is called) अयं this अपि च also प्रबुद्धानां of the enlightened प्राणसंयम: the control of the vital force (i. e. Prânâyâma) (भवति is) अज्ञानां of the ignorant घ्राणपीडनम् pressing of the nose (भवति is).

119-120. The negation of the phenomenal world is known as Rechaka (breathing out), the thought, "I am verily Brahman," is called Puraka (breathing in), and the steadiness of that thought thereafter is called Kumbhaka (restraining the breath). This is the real course of

Prânâyâma[1] for the enlightened, whereas the
ignorant only torture the nose.

[1] *Prânâyâma*—Patanjali describes it as "controlling the
motion of the exhalation and the inhalation" (II.49). There
are three steps in it. The first step is to draw in the breath
(Puraka), the next is to hold it for some time in the lungs
(Kumbhaka), and the last is to throw it out (Rechaka).
Patanjali holds that the mind will be naturally controlled if
its communications with the external world are cut off by
restraining the breath. But Sankara here maintains that the
breath is entirely dependent on the mind and not *vice versa;*
so that instead of frittering away one's energy in the attempt
of restraining the breath one should always try to control the
mind. When this is accomplished, the restraint of the breath
will follow as a matter of course.

विषयेष्वात्मतां दृष्ट्वा मनसश्चितिमज्जनम् ।
प्रत्याहारः स विज्ञेयोऽभ्यसनीयो मुमुक्षुभिः ॥ १२१ ॥

विषयेषु In all objects आत्मतां selfhood दृष्ट्वा realizing मनस:
of the mind चिति in the supereme Consciousness मज्जनम्
absorption (इति this) प्रत्याहार: Pratyâhara विज्ञेय: is to be
known स: that मुमुक्षुभि: by the seekers after liberation
अभ्यसनीय: should be practised.

121. The absorption of the mind in the
supreme Consciousness by realizing Âtman in all
objects is known as Pratyâhâra[1] (withdrawal of
the mind) which should be practised by the
seekers after liberation.

[1] *Pratyâhâra*—"When the senses giving up their own
objects take the form of the mind, as it were, it is Pratyâhâra" (Patanjali, II.54). But its consummation is reached
only when the mind also is absorbed in the supreme Consciousness.

यत्र यत्र मनो याति ब्रह्मणस्तत्र दर्शनात् ।
मनसो धारणं चैव धारणा सा परा मता ॥ १२२ ॥

यत्र यत्र Wherever मन: the mind याति goes तत्र there
ब्रह्मण: of Brahman दर्शनात् by realization मनस: of the mind
धारणं fixing सा that एव alone च (expletive) परा supreme धारणा
Dhâranâ मता is known.

122. The steadiness of the mind through
realization of Brahman wherever the mind goes,
is known as the supreme Dhârana[1] (concentration).

[1] *The supreme Dhârana*—" Dhâranâ," says Patanjali,
" is holding the mind on to some particular object " (III.1).
But when the mind is fully concentrated on every object it
comes in contact with, realizing it as Brahman and discarding
the names and forms that have been superimposed on it by
ignorance, then alone one is said to have reached the culmination of Dhâranâ.

ब्रह्मैवास्मीति सद्वृत्त्या निरालम्बतया स्थिति: ।
ध्यानशब्देन विख्याता परमानन्ददायिनी ॥ १२३ ॥

(अहं I) ब्रह्म Brahman एव alone अस्मि am इति सद्वृत्त्या
by such unassailable thought निरालम्बतया depending on
nothing स्थिति: remaining ध्यानशब्देन by the word Dhyâna
विख्याता well known (सा this) परमानन्ददायिनी productive of
supreme bliss (भवति is).

123. Remaining independent of everything
as a result of the unassailable thought, "I am
verily Brahman," is well known by the word
Dhyânâ[1] (meditation), and is productive of
supreme bliss.

[1] *Dhyâna*—" An unbroken flow of thought in some particular object is Dhyâna " (Patanjali, III.2). But it is perfected only when one merges all thought in Brahman, realizing It to be one's own self.

निर्विकारतया वृत्तया ब्रह्माकारतया पुनः ।
वृत्तिविस्मरणं सम्यक् समाधिर्ज्ञानसंज्ञकः ॥ १२४ ॥

वृत्तया Of thought निर्विकारतया through changelessness पुनः again ब्रह्माकारतया through identification with Brahman सम्यक् complete वृत्तिविस्मरणम् forgetfulness of all mental activity (इति this) समाधिः Samâdhi (उच्यते is called) (अयं this) ज्ञानसंज्ञकः called knowledge.

124. The complete forgetfulness of all thought by first making it changeless and then identifying it with Brahman is called Samâdhi known also as knowledge.[1]

[1] *Known also as knowledge*—Samâdhi is by no means a state of unconsciousness. Notwithstanding the absence of all objective thoughts in it, the pure Consciousness is always there. To deny the presence of consciousness in any state is a sheer impossibility; since it is the very self of the person who denies it. Samâdhi is, therefore, rightly called knowledge.

इमञ्चाकृत्रिमानन्दं तावत् साधु समभ्यसेत् ।
वश्यो यावत् क्षणात् पुंसः प्रयुक्तः सन् भवेत् स्वयं ॥ १२५ ॥

(साधकः The aspirant) इमं this अकृत्रिमानन्दं (manifestor of) uncreated bliss च (expletive) तावत् so long साधु perfectly समभ्यसेत् should practise यावत् till पुंसः of the person वश्यः being under control प्रयुक्तः सन् being called into action क्षणात् in an instant स्वयं spontaneously भवेत् arises.

125. The aspirant should carefully practise this (meditation) that reveals his natural bliss until, being under his full control, it arises spontaneously, in an instant when called into action.

ततः साधननिर्मुक्तः सिद्धो भवति योगिराट् ।
ततस्वरूपं न चैतस्य विषयो मनसो गिराम् ॥ १२६ ॥

ततः Then योगिराट् the best among Yogis सिद्धः (सन्) being perfected साधननिर्मुक्तः free from all practices भवति becomes एतस्य of this(man of realization) तत् that खरूपं the real nature मनसः of the mind गिराम् of speech च also विषयः object न not (भवति becomes).

126. Then he, the best among Yogis having attained to perfection, becomes free from all practices.[1] The real nature of such a man[2] never becomes an object of the mind or speech.

[1] *Becomes free from all practices*—The various practices prescribed here and elsewhere are merely means to the realization of one's own unity with Brahman, and are no longer necessary when such realization has been accomplished. The Gitâ also declares, "For one who has been well established in Yoga, inaction is said to be the way" (VI.3).

[2] *The real nature of such a man*—The Sruti declares, "He who realizes the Supreme Brahman verily becomes Brahman" (*Mund.* III.ii.9). His nature also merges in that of Brahman "which is beyond mind and speech" (*Taitt.* II.9).

समाधौ क्रियमाणे तु विघ्नान्यायान्ति वै बलात् ।
अनुसन्धानराहित्यमालस्यं भोगलालसम् ॥ १२७॥
लयस्तमश्चविक्षेपो रसास्वादश्च शून्यता ।
एवं यद्विघ्नबाहुल्यं त्याज्यं ब्रह्मविदा शनैः ॥ १२८ ॥

समाधौ क्रियमाणे While Samâdhi (concentration) is being practised तु (expletive) अनुसन्धानराहित्यम् lack of inquiry आलस्यं idleness भोगलालसं desire for sense-enjoyment लय: sleep तम: dullness विक्षेप: distraction रसास्वाद: tasting of joy शून्यता blankness च also विघ्नानि obstacles वै indeed बलात् perforce आयान्ति appear एवं such यत् which विघ्नबाहुल्यं multiplicity of obstacles तत् that ब्रह्मविदा by the seeker after Brahman शनै: slowly त्याज्यं should be avoided.

127-28. While practising Samâdhi there appear unavoidably many obstacles, such as lack of inquiry, idleness, desire for sense-pleasure, sleep, dullness, distraction, tasting of joy,[1] and the sense of blankness.[2] One desiring the knowledge of Brahman should slowly get rid of such innumerable obstacles.

[1] *Tasting of joy*—After some progress is made in the path of spirituality there arises in the mind of the aspirant a kind of pleasurable feeling as a result of concentration. This, however, greatly hinders his spiritual progress, as it robs him of all enthusiasm for further practice.

[2] *The sense of blankness*—This is a state of mental torpidity resulting from a conflict of desires.

भाववृत्तया हि भावत्वं शून्यवृत्तया हि शून्यता ।
ब्रह्मवृत्तया हि पूर्णत्वं तथा पूर्णत्वमभ्यसेत् ॥ १२६ ॥

भाववृत्तया By the thought of an object हि verily भावत्वं identification with the object (भवति arises) शून्यवृत्त्या by the thought of a void हि verily शून्यता indentification with the void (भवति arises) ब्रह्मवृत्त्या by the thought of Brahman पूर्णत्वं perfection हि verily (भवति arises) तथा so पूर्णत्वम् perfection अभ्यसेत् should practise (जन: a person).

129. While thinking of an object the mind verily identifies itself with that, and while thinking of a void it really becomes blank, whereas by the thought of Brahman it attains to perfection. So one should constantly think of[1] (Brahman to attain) perfection.

[1] *One should constantly think of, etc.*—Whatever one thinks one becomes. So one desiring to attain to perfection should leave aside all thought of duality and fix one's mind upon the non-dual Brahman which alone is perfect.

ये हि वृत्ति जहत्येनां ब्रह्माख्यां पावनीं पराम् ।
वृथैव ते तु जीवन्ति पशुभिश्च समा नराः ॥ १३० ॥

ये Who हि (expletive) एनां this परां supremely पावनीं purifying ब्रह्माख्यां वृत्ति the thought of Brahman जहति give up ते those नराः persons तु (expletive) वृथैव in vain जीवन्ति live पशुभिः to beasts च also समाः equal (भवन्ति are).

130. Those who give up this supremely purifying thought of Brahman, live in vain and are on the same level with beasts.[1]

[1] *On the same level with beasts*—Man has the unique opportunity of realizing Brahman and thus becoming free from the bondage of ignorance. But if he does not avail himself of this opportunity, he can hardly be called a man, as there remains nothing to distinguish him from the lower animals.

ये हि वृत्ति विजानन्ति ज्ञात्वापि वर्धयन्ति ये ।
ते वै सत्पुरुषा धन्या वन्द्यास्ते भुवनत्रये ॥ १३१ ॥

ये Who सत्पुरुषाः virtuous persons हि (expletive) वृत्ति the consciousness (of Brahman) विजानन्ति know ज्ञात्वा knowing अपि and ये who (तां that) वर्धयन्ति develop ते those वै indeed

धन्या: blessed (भवन्ति are) ते they भुवनत्रये in the three worlds
वन्द्या: respected (भवन्ति are).

131. Blessed indeed are those virtuous persons who at first have this consciousness of Brahman[1] and then develop it more and more. They are respected everywhere.

[1] *Have this consciousness of Brahman, etc.*—After long practice, the aspirant at first realizes, while in Samâdhi, the presence of Brahman which pervades the inner and the outer world. But this is not all. He should then hold on this Brahmic consciousness until he feels his identity with Brahman at every moment and thus becomes completely free from the bonds of all duality and ignorance. This is the consummation of spiritual practice.

येषां वृत्तिः समा वृद्धा परिपक्वा च सा पुनः ।
ते वै सद्ब्रह्मतां प्राप्ता नेतरे शब्दवादिनः ॥ १३२ ॥

येषां Whose वृत्ति: consciousness (of Brahman) समा same वृद्धा developed सा that च also पुन: again परिपक्वा mature ते they वै alone सद्ब्रह्मतां the state of ever-existent Brahman प्राप्ता: have attained to इतरे others शब्दवादिन: those who dabble in words न not.

132. Only those in whom this consciousness[1] (of Brahman) being ever present grows into maturity, attain to the state of ever-existent Brahman; and not others who merely deal with words.[2]

[1] *This consciousness*—that Brahman alone is the reality pervading our whole being.

[2] *Deal with words*—Engage themselves in fruitless discussions about Brahman by variously interpreting texts bearing upon It.

कुशला ब्रह्मवार्तायां वृत्तिहीनाः सुरागिणः ।
तेऽप्यज्ञानतया नूनं पुनरायान्ति यान्ति च ॥ १३३ ॥

ये Those ब्रह्मवार्तायां in discussing about Brahman कुशला:
clever वृत्तिहीना: devoid of the consciousness (of Brahman)
(तु but) सुरागिण: very much attached to (worldly pleasures)
ते they अपि also अज्ञानतया on account of their ignorance नूनं
surely पुन: again and again आयान्ति come यान्ति go च and.

133. Also those persons who are only clever
in discussing about Brahman but have no realization, and are very much attached to worldly
pleasures, are born and die again and again in
consequence of their ignorance.

निमेषार्धं न तिष्ठन्ति वृत्तिं ब्रह्ममयीं विना ।
यथा तिष्ठन्ति ब्रह्माद्याः सनकाद्याः शुकादयः ॥ १३४ ॥

(साधका: The aspirants) ब्रह्ममयीं imbued with Brahman
वृत्तिं thought विना without निमेषार्धं half an instant न not तिष्ठन्ति
stay यथा just as ब्रह्माद्या: Brahmâ and others सनकाद्या: Sanaka
and others शुकादय: Suka and others (न not) तिष्ठन्ति remain.

134. The aspirant after Brahman should not
remain[1] a single moment without the thought of
Brahman, just like Brahmâ, Sanaka, Suka and
others.

[1] *Should not remain, etc.*—To be ever immersed in the
Brahmic consciousness and thus identify oneself with It is the
final aim of Râja-Yoga.

[With this verse ends the exposition of Râja-Yoga in
the light of Vedânta.

We may mention here in passing that although there is
no vital difference between Râja-Yoga as expounded here and
as found in the Yoga-sutras of Patanjali so far as the final

realization is concerned, yet there is much difference in the
practices. Patanjali has prescribed the control of the body
and Prâna prior to the practice of meditation, whereas the
author here emphasizes the meditation of Brahman from the
very beginning and thus wants to lead the aspirant straight to
the goal.]

कार्ये कारणतायाता कारणे नहि कार्यता ।
कारणत्वं ततो गच्छेत् कार्याभावे विचारतः ॥ १३५ ॥

कार्ये In the effect कारणता the nature of the cause आयाता
inheres कारणे in the cause कार्यता the nature of the effect न
not हि verily ततः therefore विचारतः through reasoning
कार्याभावे in the absence of the effect कारणत्वं the causality
गच्छेत् disappears.

135. The nature of the cause inheres in the
effect and not *vice versa;* so through reasoning it
is found that in the absence of the effect[1] the
cause, as such, also disappears.

[1] *In the absence of the effect, etc.*—The cause and the
effect are correlative; as long as there is an effect there is a
cause for it. But when the effect is altogether absent, the
cause, as such, can no longer exist, as there remains nothing
with reference to which it may be called a cause.

अथ शुद्धं भवेद्वस्तु यद्वै वाचामगोचरम् ।
द्रष्टव्यं मृद्घटेनैव दृष्टान्तेन पुनः पुनः ॥ १३६ ॥

अथ Then यत् which वै indeed शुद्धं pure वाचां of words
अगोचरं beyond the range वस्तु reality (तत् that) भवेत्
remains मृद्घटेन of earth and the pot दृष्टान्तेन through the
illustration एव verily (तत् that) पुनः पुनः again and again
द्रष्टव्यं should be understood.

136. Then that pure reality (Brahman) which is beyond speech alone remains. This should be understood again and again verily through the illustration of earth and the pot.[1]

[1] *The illustration of earth and the pot*—The illustration runs thus: " Just as, my dear, by knowing a lump of earth everything made of earth is known—the modifications are mere names originated by speech, earth alone is the reality," etc. (*Chhând. Up.* VI.i.4). Here also the phenomenal world exists only in name, Brahman alone is the reality.

अनेनैव प्रकारेण वृत्तिर्ब्रह्मात्मिका भवेत् ।
उदेति शुद्धचित्तानां वृत्तिज्ञानं ततः परम् ॥ १३७ ॥

अनेनैव प्रकारेण In this very way शुद्धचित्तानां of the pure-minded वृत्तिज्ञानम् a state of awareness (of Brahman) उदेति arises ततः परं thereafter (सा that) वृत्तिः mental state ब्रह्मात्मिका imbued with Brahman भवेत् becomes.

137. In this way alone[1] there arises in the pure-minded a state of awareness (of Brahman), which is afterwards merged into Brahman.

[1] *In this way alone, etc.*—By constant practice of contemplation and discrimination there dawns on the mind of the aspirant the knowledge that Brahman alone is, and nothing else exists. Thus the ignorance which has so long deluded him by projecting the world of duality, comes to an end. Thereafter the mind also, which by destroying ignorance has brought the aspirant so close to Brahman, vanishes like the fire which after consuming its fuel is itself extinguished, then Brahman alone shines in Its own glory.

कारणं व्यतिरेकेण पुमानादौ विलोकयेत् ।
अन्वयेन पुनस्तद्धि कार्ये नित्यं प्रपश्यति ॥ १३८ ॥

पुमान् A person आदौ at first व्यतिरेकेण by the negative method कारणं the cause विलोकयेत् should examine पुन: again तत् that (i.e. cause) हि verily अन्वयेन by the positive method कार्ये in the effect नित्यं ever प्रपश्यति understands.

138. One should[1] first look for the cause by the negative method and then find it by the positive method, as ever inherent in the effect.

[1] *One should, etc.*—The cause can be inferred either from a positive or from a negative proposition. The positive proposition is : " Where there is an effect, there must be a cause "; and the negative one is : " Where there is no cause, there is no effect." From either proposition we come to the conclusion that there is Brahman which is the cause of the world-phenomenon. For, if there were no Brahman (cause), there would be no world at all; again, there is the world (effect), therefore there is Brahman (cause).

कार्यं हि कारणं पश्येत् पश्चात् कार्यं विसर्जयेत् ।
कारणत्वं ततो गच्छेद्वशिष्टं भवेन्मुनिः ॥ १३९ ॥

कार्ये In the effect कारणं the cause हि verily पश्येत् should see पश्चात् afterwards कार्यं the effect विसर्जयेत् should dismiss तत: then कारणत्वं the causality गच्छेत् goes away मुनि: the sage अवशिष्टं the residue भवेत् becomes.

139. One should verily see the cause in the effect, and then dismiss the effect altogether. What then remains,[1] the sage himself becomes.

[An alternative method is suggested here.]

[1] *What then remains, etc.*—When both cause and effect have thus disappeared one may naturally conclude that only Sunya, a void, is left behind. But it is not so. For absolute negation is an impossibility. One may negate everything but cannot negate one's own Self. So when causality has been

negated, what is beyond all negation is the very Self of the enquirer, which is the ultimate reality.

भावितं तीव्रवेगेन यद्वस्तु निश्चयात्मना ।
पुमांस्तद्धि भवेच्छीघ्रं ज्ञेयं भ्रमरकीटवत् ॥ १४० ॥

निश्चयात्मना With firm conviction तीव्रवेगेन most energetically यत् that वस्तु thing भावितं is meditated upon पुमान् a person तत् that हि verily शीघ्रं quickly भवेत् becomes (एतत् this) भ्रमरकीटवत् from the illustration of the wasp and the insect ज्ञेयं should be understood.

140. A person who meditates upon a thing with great assiduity and firm conviction, becomes that very thing. This may be understood[1] from the illustration of the wasp and the worm.

[1] *This may be understood, etc.*—It is a popular belief that when a wasp brings into its hole a particular kind of insect, the latter, out of fear, constantly thinks of its assailant till it is transformed into a wasp. So also if a person meditates upon Brahman with all his mind, he will become Brahman in course of time.

अदृश्यं भावरूपञ्च सर्वमेव चिदात्मकम् ।
सावधानतया नित्यं स्वात्मानं भावयेद्बुधः ॥ १४१ ॥

बुधः The wise अदृश्यं the invisible भावरूपं the substantial (i. e. the visible) च also सर्वं everything चिदात्मकं of the nature of consciousness स्वात्मानं as one's own Self एव verily सावधानतया with great care नित्यं always भावयेत् should think of.

141. The wise should always think with great care of the invisible, the visible and everything else, as his own Self which is consciousness itself.

दृश्यं हादृश्यतां नीत्वा ब्रह्माकारेण चिन्तयेत् ।
विद्वान्नित्यसुखे तिष्ठेद्धिया चिद्रसपूर्णया ॥ १४२ ॥

विद्वान् The wise दृश्यं the visible हि (expletive) अदृश्यतां to invisibility नीत्वा reducing ब्रह्माकारेण as Brahman चिन्तयेत् should think of (ततः then) चिद्रसपूर्णया full of consciousness and bliss धिया with the mind नित्यसुखे in eternal felicity तिष्ठेत् should abide in.

142. Having reduced the visible[1] to the invisible, the wise should think of the universe as one with Brahman. Thus alone will he abide in eternal felicity with the mind full of consciousness and bliss.

[1] *Having reduced the visible, etc.*—A person may at first take some external thing as an object of his meditation, but he should afterwards think of it as existing only in the form of the mind; and lastly the mind also should be reduced to Brahman which is pure consciousness. Then alone one is said to have reached the highest goal.

एभिरङ्गैः समायुक्तो राजयोग उदाहृतः ।
किञ्चित्पक्ककषायाणां हठयोगेन संयुतः ॥ १४३ ॥

एभिरङ्गैः With these steps समायुक्तः fitted राजयोगः Râja-Yoga उदाहृतः has been described किञ्चित्पक्ककषायाणां for those whose worldly desires are partially consumed हठयोगेन with Hatha-Yoga (अयं this) संयुतः combined (भवेत् should be).

143. Thus has been described Râja-Yoga consisting of these steps[1] (mentioned above). With this is to be combined Hatha-Yoga[2] for (the benefit of) those whose worldly desires are partially attenuated.

[1] *These steps*—The fifteen steps mentioned in verses 100-134.

[2] *With this is to be combined Hatha-Yoga, etc.*—This Râja-Yoga, which is purely psychological in its character, is extremely difficult to be practised by those who have not yet overcome the physical disabilities and banished the carnal appetites from the mind and thus made it pure. To them, therefore, Hatha-Yoga, or the Yoga that teaches physical control together with a little concentration, is at first very helpful. For, they may thereby get control over their external and internal nature and thus may in course of time become fit for the practice of this Râja-Yoga.

परिपक्कं मनो येषां केवलोऽयं च सिद्धिदः ।
गुरुदैवतभक्तानां सर्वेषां सुलभो जवात् ॥ १४४ ॥

येषां Whose मनः mind परिपक्कं completely mature, i. e. free from impurities (तेषां for them) केवलोऽयं this alone च (expletive) सिद्धिदः productive of the highest result (i. e. perfection) (भवति is) गुरुदैवतभक्तानां to those devoted to the teacher and the Deity सर्वेषां of all (तत् that) जवात् speedily सुलभः easy to achieve (भवति becomes).

144. For those whose mind is completely purified this (Râja-Yoga) alone is productive of perfection. Purity of the mind, again, is speedily accessible to those who are devoted[1] to the teacher and the Deity.

[1] *Those who are devoted, etc.*—Those who have implicit faith in the words of the Guru and have unflinching devotion to their chosen Deity, become free from all doubts and thus easily acquire concentration which directly leads them to the realization of the highest truth.